THE CAT THAT COULD OPEN THE FRIDGE

The Cat that

Could Open the Fridge

A CURMUDGEON'S GUIDE TO
CHRISTMAS ROUND ROBIN LETTERS

Simon Hoggart

Atlantic Books
London

Published in hardback in Great Britain in 2004 by Atlantic Books.
Atlantic Books is an imprint of Grove Atlantic Ltd.

The author and publisher gratefully acknowledge the
following for permission to reproduce:
'Christmas Circulars' © Carole Satyamurti, 1990

ISBN 1 84354 357 5

9   8   7   6   5   4   3

Printed in Great Britain by CPD, Ebbw Vale, Wales.
Text design by Lindsay Nash

Atlantic Books
An imprint of Grove Atlantic Ltd
Ormond House
26–27 Boswell Street
London
WC1N 3JZ

Contents

Introduction

THE APPARENTLY PUZZLING title of this book is easy to explain. In 2003 I received a classic example of the round robin genre. It consisted of two closely typed sheets of A4 paper, including nearly 2,000 words in all. The first page was a lengthy and detailed description of all the medical disasters the couple who had sent the letter had suffered throughout the year. As you will see, later in this book, these were numerous and unpleasant. This was followed by fairly neutral material – holidays and trips, some good, others bad – until the very end, where they revealed that they had bought a new, large fridge. Unfortunately their cat had learned to open it, and I thought how awful it was to suffer so much in the course of the year, then to end it with every pet owner's nightmare – the cat or dog that can help itself. It also struck me as very funny, but we'll come to that later.

Nobody knows when the first circular Christmas letters appeared. It is hardly likely that cavemen sent them – not because every member of the clan already knew every detail of the lives of every other member of the clan (that would not stop most of the people who appear in this book) but because the technology wasn't there. Drawing pictures of yourself hunting a bison or inventing the wheel ('Tharg is pretty popular at work these days. His bosses say his new invention may have real possibilities, such as rolling at mastodons!') might be a pleasant means of boasting. But it couldn't be duplicated. The first person in this country capable of producing a circular letter was William Caxton (1422–91), who set up the first British printing press, at Westminster.

So far as we know he didn't. But he could have done. Or got his wife to write it. ('Well, friends, one and all, near and far! 1476 has been a busy year for the Caxtons!!! As you would know from last year's letter, if we had had the means of sending one, Bill acquired the UK franchise for the exciting new German "printing" process, which seems to take up all his free time – at least it means he can't help with the shopping – can you hear the sound of me nagging??? Moi??? Luckily he has a great assistant, so take a bow, Wynkyn de Worde. Crazy name, crazy guy!!!')

For centuries, unless you had your own press, the circular letter was pretty much an impossibility. You could type half a dozen letters at once using carbon paper, but the last few were almost illegible. Things changed with the arrival of the Gestetner machine, which made 'stencils', sheets of a fibrous paper-like material with an inked backing that let you see what you were typing. If you made a mistake, you had to cover it with a plastic sort of fluid, and type over that. The result looked like a chicken pox victim's face. Then you mounted the stencil on an inked drum, turned a handle like a mangle, and limitless blodgy, smudged, inky, smeary copies spewed out, all ready to send to your 200 dearest friends. ('Jo ny had s me good n ws in N vember') If you had access to a Gestetner, that is, and nobody had them at home.

I can't remember when I was last sent a stencilled letter. There must be landfills of Gestetners somewhere or other, like reel-to-reel tape-recorders and Grundig video-recorders. No doubt it will turn out that the ink they used will poison the water table.

The next great advance in the world of round robins was the photocopier (and please don't write to say that a 'round robin' was originally a petition of complaint on board ships in the eighteenth century, the point of its circular shape being that the ring-leader could not be identified and flogged. I know that, but words change their meaning, and everyone now knows what a 'round robin' means.)

The photocopier was simpler. You could type the document at home, sneak it into the office, and use your lunch hour to run off 150 copies in ten minutes. The hazard for the Xerox user was that you might get caught and your boss could demand payment for all that paper. The machines were always breaking down, with the hot news about Tamsin's ten starred GCSEs stuck in a paper jam. Most likely of all, you could forget the original, and leave it in the machine, the source of much ribaldry and jeering from your col-leagues. You might think that this experience, or the fear of it, would so horrify the writers that they would anticipate a similar reaction from their intended recipients. This does not seem to have happened very often.

The growth in the number of small shops offering photocopying, sometimes for as little as 3p a sheet, made this technology open even to people who didn't work in offices. And it saved money too. Few Christmas cards cost much less than 39p each, and of course a letter is so much more personal. And offers far more opportunity to boast, or list in detail all the horrors in your life.

It's the home computer that has really made the round robin ubiquitous. Clearly it's the simplest way of producing multitudinous copies, but these can now be gussied up to a remarkable extent. It is not unusual these days to get a letter that includes several pages of misery – emergency operations, dead relatives, sackings, disastrous holidays and so forth – decorated with jolly snowmen, chirpy robins and smiling Santas. Sometimes people go much, much further. One family in London – they know who they are – send out an entire booklet of around thirty-two pages, listing every place they have visited, the historical significance of the buildings they have seen, and the political situation in each country – from, it must be said, a traditional left-wing standpoint. This isn't a seasonal greeting, but 'what we did in the hols' merged with a political tract. It's so unremitting that you can't help thinking that George W. Bush can't be all that bad if he is disliked by these people. Length is a hazard. Later in this book you will find an extract from a Christmas letter sent out by a Scottish academic to all his former pupils. The full text is, I estimate, 39,000 words – as long as some novels – and actually includes a separate sheet of footnotes.

Computers have also made it possible to include photographs, which used to look very smudgy on a photocopy. There is something quite infuriating about seeing a small picture of an entire family eating quiche under a tree in Provence, or waving their wine glasses at you from a hot tub in New Zealand. These snaps are far more annoying than anything that appears in the travel supplements. The newspaper pictures imply 'you could do this'. The circular letters say smugly 'we already have'.

I first became aware of the circular letter in the early 1960s. My father, a university professor, had an academic colleague whom he knew very slightly. This man had married an American artist. Many years later he emigrated to Washington where, during a spell as a reporter there, I came to know and to like him very much. But every time he opened his mouth, I was wafted back to my childhood, when he and his wife had sent us one of those thin, floppy plastic records that you could make privately for not a lot of money, and which some magazines gave away with the Christmas number.

Previously they had sent sticks of rock and other amusing gifts. This record, however, consisted of them reading out their 'family alphabet', and the brash American voice of the New York artist alternating with the more diffident tones of a British lecturer was beguiling. ('B is for Brighton, and bracing, balmy breezes!'; 'E is for England, for ours truly is a green and pleasant land!'; 'S is for Suzie, sweet sixteen and sure to find a sweetheart!') Of particular delight to me and my family were two letters near the end: 'V is for Vietnam. Peace on its tired earth!' and, stuck with the problem faced by every compiler of alphabets, the letter X: 'X is for xenophobia. A pox on it!'

Whenever my siblings and I hear either of those words in each other's company, and sometimes, bafflingly for them, other people's company, our reaction is immediate. 'I hear Jack and Sophie are having their honeymoon in Vietnam,' someone will say, and we add gravely, 'peace on its tired earth!', getting the inflections just right. As for 'xenophobia' or any of its variants, you can guess. It still makes us laugh immoderately.

Two years after the alphabet we got a simple card. The front showed the wife and children in a revolving door, and was labelled 'A New Beginning'. You opened it, and in the place where you'd expect a to find a greeting was only the legend, 'Max and I have separated'. It was the last time we ever heard from them; we were dropped from their Rolodex. But I miss that tough, take-no-prisoners style of round robins.

Why do people hate these letters? Not everyone does. When people send them in to me every year at the *Guardian*, I study the covering note almost as closely as the actual letter. Some are filled with loathing: 'I hate these people, hate them, hate them, hate them!' is not untypical. Others clearly get a great sense of relief, of closure, at getting them out of their house. ('My wastepaper basket is too good for this,' one reader wrote.) Other people, by contrast, enjoy getting them. Quite a few readers, slightly hurt by my comments, send in their own round robins and ask me to approve them.

So what's wrong with circular letters? Lots of things, really. There is often far too much detail (see the chapter on this topic, which provides some chilling examples). If you live next door to the writers, or see them several times a year, or are part of their family, you already know all that stuff. If, however, you are someone who met the husband twenty years ago at a conference in Derby and have never set eyes on him since, and never met his wife or his children, then you simply don't want to know it. It's a pretty narrow spectrum of one's acquaintance who actually require all this material.

Also, the writers tend to be terribly selective. One *Guardian* reader told me in a covering note: 'You would think that these people are blissfully happy. In fact the wife is permanently on tranquillizers' – a point made vividly in Carole Satyamurti's poem, reproduced later in this book.

The letters can also seem immensely intrusive. Why should you be force-fed information about Tamsin's success in her exams, or the new conservatory, or that fabulous villa in Umbria? Why should I take in this stuff about Roger's decision to cycle to work for health reasons, or the family trip to Barbados, or the new pet rabbit? If it were true that for every new fact your brain admits, another is forced out, then vital data are having to make way for the news that somebody's book group has been reading *The Life of Pi* or that someone you can barely remember almost missed their flight to Antwerp because the taxi was delayed.

Smugness is the main complaint from my readers. Often a letter will consist of elements that, on their own, would be unexceptional: holidays, family gatherings, children's activities and so forth. It's the cumulative effect that makes teeth grind. Doesn't anything go wrong in these people's lives? Sometimes it's faintly hinted at: 'Work has not gone quite as well as hoped... but with an upturn expected in the industry, who knows what next year will bring?'

For some people *everything* does go wrong, often on a spectacular scale. Here I must confess to a sense of guilt. As you will see from the chapter on disasters, bad news doesn't come in threes – it comes in twenty-threes, or 103s. And there is, I regret to say, something hilarious about the cumulative misfortunes of somebody you don't know. I can't say why this is. If it were someone you were close to, you'd be appalled. 'The Pettigrews have had an awful time,' you would say sympathetically to your partner, who might lie awake worrying about them all night. But when it's strangers inflicting every detail of their misfortunes upon you, then I'm afraid it becomes funny. This may tell you more about me than about human nature in general, but I have to say that most people I know share my view.

On the other hand, minor mishaps can usually be blamed on other people. Builders who never turn up. Infuriating neighbours. A garage that can't or won't fix your car. A boss who suffers from self-esteem issues and never gives Julian the space he needs to develop. There's a cloying sense of dishonesty hanging over some of the letters. Do these people really spend their spare time on charity work and restoring antique musical instruments? Why does nobody ever write: 'Terry, as ever, spent most evenings in the pub, while I slumped in front of the television with a microwave pizza. I really love *Heartbeat* and *The Bill.*' Or, 'running bring-and-buy sales for UKIP really keeps us on our toes!'

Whole areas of life are missing. Sex, for instance, almost never gets a mention. You do not read, 'after moving to our little village, we were delighted to learn that wife-swapping parties are a major feature of the local social life'. It's never even hinted at. No one writes, 'so far Matthew is without a brother or sister, but you can imagine we're having plenty of fun trying to remedy that!'

There are certain big mistakes the people who write these letters should always avoid. Never write in verse. Even if you think you can do the job properly, you are almost certain to wind up writing something like: 'A somewhat rainy weekend was passed in west Cornwall / Where, thanks to our cosy caravan, we had no worries at all.' I beg you, just don't do it.

It's also a grievous mistake to arrange your year chronologically. This can lead to alarming juxtapositions: 'April: Peter took advantage of the dry weather to replace the guttering around the house. Not before time, said Annie! May: After a long illness, borne bravely and stoically, Peter's mother died in her old people's home…' (It is surprising how often news of the death of an elderly member of the family will crop up halfway through an otherwise jaunty letter. I suppose it's because very few people want to kick off by saying, 'this year will always remain sadly in our memory because we lost my beloved father in a tragic and wholly unnecessary car crash', though a minority of people do just that. On the other hand, squeezing it in between the new conservatory and Angie's part-time job at Café Rouge just looks heartless.)

Religion should be avoided. Not the 'we often help out at the church' type of religion, or, 'we hope to attend an ecumenical gathering in Cologne next year,' but the proselytizing to which Americans are especially prone. It's odd how often letters that begin with an invocation of the deity – 'our Lord, whose tender care we sense and acknowledge every day of our lives' – end with a series of horrors to which the same Lord seems surprisingly indifferent, such as an incurable illness or a tragic accident. In the holiday season of 2001–02, many readers sent in letters that attempted to analyse God's failure to prevent the attacks of 9/11.

Americans, of course – and Europeans too, to a slightly lesser extent – tend to believe that when bad things happen to Americans it is worse than in any other country. Thousands can die when a dam bursts in China but His motivation for allowing that to happen is never explored. One letter quoted in this book explains how on 9/11 God was not asleep at the switch. Instead He was organizing traffic jams to slow people getting to the World Trade Center, and to Logan Airport where the hijacked planes took off from. This may be a plausible explanation to true believers, but deeply wounding to anyone whose loved ones sailed through the traffic. Sometimes His successes are more modest. There's a wonderful account in this book of a woman who suffered from anorexia. She was encouraged to go to a certain church in Yorkshire, where she prayed. On her way home, she felt pangs of hunger, and ate an entire Eccles cake she bought at a petrol station. Truly the Lord moves in mysterious ways, at least for the writers of circular letters.

People quite often ask me if *all* round robins are intolerable, and of course the answer is no. We have good friends who went to live in Ireland, and their annual letter is an excellent way to keep in touch. We know all the members of the family, so it's easy to picture their lives. If we lived next door, or hadn't set eyes on them for twenty years, it would be intolerable.

But it may be too late for the circular letter. Mockery in the press and on the radio has made people more wary. *Guardian* readers in particular sometimes find their correspondents asking them not to send the letter to me. Many do anyway – it may be a useful reminder – but I assume quite a number stick to the request. I get a lot of spoof letters sent these days, and people are rather proud of them, though some try a little too hard. ('Charles was delighted to find that his cure for cancer had passed all tests with flying colours, just after he returned from his one-man trip to the summit of Mount Everest. I hope to conduct the LSO this March in a difficult work by Shostakovich…') But there are plenty in the old style: boasting, whingeing, cheerful and miserable, philosophical and nit-picking, testy and grandiloquent, packed with facts without information and information without knowledge, often blissfully lacking in self-awareness.

At the same time, I do feel a sneaking sense of admiration for many of these people. Even if half of what they write is true, and even if it is a sanitized version of their lives, which, like everyone else's, is bound to involve pain, unhappiness, failure and embarrassment, as well as a great deal of time on the couch gazing at a television – it has to be said that the British middle classes are astonishingly active and resilient. No sooner have they finished raising money for the church than they're off on a camping holiday in Cornwall, or doing a course in Moroccan pottery, or building a conservatory, or organizing a family reunion, or persuading their hapless children to learn the clavichord. The energy, the resource, the sheer get-up-and-go both appal and impress.

All the extracts from letters that follow are absolutely genuine, sent in to me by recipients, and in a handful of cases, by the original writers. As the saying goes, you couldn't make them up; nothing fictional could convey the blend of horror, smugness, self-satisfaction, misfortune and sheer exuberance. I have, however, changed all the names – usually to a substitute that conveys the age, class and – sometimes – parental eccentricity. I have also changed almost all places, except where the location is necessary for the full flavour of the letter to emerge. And if you get some prime examples, please send them to me, c/o the publisher. I feel a second volume coming on.

A Little Diamond to Polish

IF THERE IS one thing that is absolutely guaranteed to enrage the recipients of round robin letters, it is news of other people's wonderful children. Why do these paragons never seem to fail their exams, throw teenage tantrums, or hang out with unsuitable friends? Why do they spend so much time on their schoolwork and their musical instruments (including, in some cases, 'flugelhorns', heaven help us), and why do they never spend time slumped in front of *Neighbours*, or a computer game? How is it they always get to their first choice university, and never have to settle for a former polytechnic because they got two Cs and a D? Surely some of them do drugs, or at least go binge-drinking? Why do they seem so much better, so much more unutterably perfect, than our own children?

Not all of them, of course, and a very few round robins include brats and teenage nightmares. But it would be hard to keep the contents of such a letter from the eyes of the children themselves, and so many writers think too much honesty might be unwise. Instead, natural parental pride and the desire of middle-class families to encourage their offspring means that we, the readers, are furnished with almost exclusively happy news. It is most people's experience of teenagers that they must be even more embarrassed by the buckets of praise tossed over them than they would be by criticism. What seventeen-year-old would risk another seventeen-year-old reading about their devotion to academic work or, come to that, the Grade V in a musical instrument played by only seven other people in the entire world?

> JACQUELINE *our eldest daughter will be ten in February. She is kind and gentle and cares for anyone who is sad… she has wonderful perception. Her sister Luciana is eight. She is a live wire — wants to be doing something every minute of every day. Art and craft are her particular passions. She has thick blonde hair with big blue eyes. She has plenty of personality and at the end of a rough or a long day her energizing hugs are the best medicine I have ever known.*

> IN MARCH, *Kati gained distinction for Grade IV theory and is currently awaiting the result of Grade V flugelhorn.*

> LEXIE *settled into school from Day One, has made crowds of friends, and is more than surviving. Academically, I caught her reading her Latin textbook the first weekend, as she wanted to know more about it… her grades have been brilliant. Poppy has just been a King in the school nativity play, which was the most brilliant nativity play I have ever seen.*

Other people are pressed in to line up and join the chorus of parental praise.

> HARVEY *was nine on August 1st, and commands serious respect at a daunting 5'2". His teachers at his primary school have nothing but praise both for his achievements and his character. He completed his Amateur Swimming Association level 12 this summer... he began trombone lessons in September and already plays in the school band. In the Christmas performance, based on themes in the 1960s, he took on the role of Bobby Moore and was an enthusiastic participant in the Sheffield peace march.*

> TIM *has made a big impression at his new school, especially on the headmaster, who keeps having him in his study for a chinwag.*

That was written without evident irony, which may say something about either Tim's behaviour or the headmaster's proclivities. Of course being the Leonardo of your day doesn't necessarily mean you walk into the finest summer jobs.

> JESSICA *got her A-levels (straight As) despite going to every party in NW London for the whole year, and has therefore got into her university of first choice, Bristol, to read Drama in 2004 — there were only two deferred places and over one thousand applicants! She even got a mention in the school newsletter! Broadway, here we come! First, she is working in W H Smith's.*

No child in these letters ever has to be dragged unwillingly to piano practice, or forced to pick up a detested musical instrument.

WHERE *to start? Let's start with little Titus who is turning into a very competent violin player. He is set for his first public performance at church over Christmas, and pleased as punch to be playing with the big ones. Terri's church music group goes from strength to strength; Ariadne and Jolyon play regularly. Jolyon has a music scholarship from the education department and if we tell you that he has a special solo playing Lisa's sax part in the Simpsons theme you'll get a feel for how much he loves to play. It seems that when he picks up his sax it's just an extension of his body. Where does Jolyon end and the music begin?*

SOPHIE *is a creature of habit, gaining a Merit in every music exam she's ever taken. This year was no exception, with Merits of Grade 5 piano and flute. She also took her first dancing exam in July with Grade 3 Tap, for which she was awarded . . . yes, a Merit, with 81 per cent. This was something of a surprise to us, as the sentence 'an elephant is a graceful bird' has always sprung to mind with her.*

HARD *to believe that Tasha will be ten on the 9th! She still enjoys swimming, and will go and do thirty lengths. She plays both the piano and the clarinet, so the words 'have you practised your piano and clarinet?' are often heard in our house.*

ALISON *has had a very musical year playing her trumpet in various bands and orchestras. She went off to Prague with a school music trip and has recently played in the Royal Festival Hall with our county schools symphony orchestra. She continues with her piano, ballet and Duke of Edinburgh award scheme, even though this is her GCSE year.*

FELICITY *is a passionate, compassionate eleven-year-old. She loves maths and sciences along with the arts and technology. She enjoys being a wandering minstrel, walking round the house, playing her violin.*

But it's never enough for these kids to be good at just one, or even three things.

MARTIN *sings so well he was made Head Chorister at school, and will be introducing the chamber choir at the concert hall in December. He is still learning the piano and flute. He still loves sport too and was delighted to hear the sports and music teachers fight over him to be Sports Captain rather than Head Chorister.*

AMBER *is now in full time school; she loves her school and literally runs to her classroom every morning. Early in the year she was awarded a merit badge for her class, and she has been chosen to play Mary in the upcoming nativity play. She will have the opportunity to sing a solo. Outside school she takes dance, music*

and swimming lessons and in her down time she always has a
marker, crayon or paint brush in her hand. Our Christmas cards
this year were entirely designed by Amber.

All that from a five-year-old. But there is no end to the talents of our writers' children.

HARRY *was 'Jesus' in the school 'Jesus Christ, Superstar'.*
This was the best production I have ever seen, youth or adult.
The organization is wonderful and all the children gain so much.
Both boys, especially Harry, were physically and emotionally
drained at the end of it. I was drained too — seeing your son
crucified nightly is not an experience I would recommend —
especially when he calls out for his mother!

When they tackle sport, these children naturally make it almost to the top.

GREG *has also been chosen for the school rugby team, partly we*
believe because he has no fear.

Some readers have sent me whole series of letters from successive years. This has enabled me, for example, to keep up with Amy's astonishing success in her girls' cricket team, with detailed descriptions, season by season, of how many runs she scored and how many wickets she took. Girls in particular are now into boys' sports.

CASSANDRA *made a great start in secondary school this year. Better than we could have hoped for. Her number one sport continues to be soccer. She also signed up for water polo, which necessitated being at the pool 7 a.m. on Monday mornings. (I was thrilled, being the morning person I am. Ha ha!) She joined the school concert band and jazz band. Having played the alto sax for ten years, she was also asked to play the tenor sax, so she heads off to band practice with a sax in each hand. She has made a lot of friends and is popular in her year… she again played soccer in two teams through the winter, with the boys' team on Saturdays and girls on Sundays. One of the boys paid her the ultimate compliment when he told his Dad 'we'll be in trouble today as Cassie won't be playing.'*

JACQUI *manages to train as a surgeon while fitting in diving trips to Thailand, Cayman, Cuba and the Red Sea. We've told you about Tori's sporting prowess, and at number 5 in the world, she is not doing badly!*

THE BOYS *have a heavy training schedule. They also have a hamster.*

The recipient wrote in the margin of that letter: 'no doubt soon to be entered in the World Hamster Wheel speed championships.' Of course these happy children do have a lot of help from their supportive, or perhaps at times oppressive, parents.

NATASHA *continues at our local university in political science. She*
is devouring history and politics and this year took on Spanish, as
she is planning a trip to Latin America next summer. To give her a
helping hand, I hired a cleaning lady from El Salvador, so she can
have some conversation practice.

Possibly learning how to shout, 'and why is my bed not made at
4 in the afternoon?' in faultless Spanish.

Not only do these children have a tremendous cultural and
intellectual life, but their diet is pretty near perfect too. No
worries about childhood obesity among these dietary paragons:

SHE IS *incredibly fit and lean, eats virtually no sweets, loves*
Granny Smith apples, and drinks loads of fruit juice.

WE MUST *have one of the most varied and healthy diets of anyone*
in the country — though chilli, coriander and ginger do tend to
turn up rather more often than potatoes. Jack and Lulu would like
to be reminded what a chip is!

Oh, I don't know. I suspect the occasional sneak visit to
McDonald's for Jack and Lulu, on the way home from school.

Sometimes there's just so much going on, it's hard to cram it
all into one letter:

IN MARCH, *Stephanie passed her Grade 5 ballet exam with flying*
colours and Richard appeared in a concert with the newly named

Compagnie des Chansons... *we were in the village production of* As You Like It. *I played Phoebe (a heartless shepherdess) and Stephanie sang beautifully... in July Stephanie passed her Grade 4 piano exam, with merit, and Peter spent his last few days at primary school. He rounded off the summer term with a snarlingly wonderful performance as the Sheriff of Nottingham. He had great fun in his solo, pushing over schoolmates and stealing flowers from little girls... in November, Peter appeared in another wonderful* Chansons *concert. Stephanie has just taken her saxophone Grade 5 — we await the results.*

And we know exactly what those results will be, without having to wait, with bated breath, for next year's letter.

It is certainly true that if the children of people who send round robins were any kind of guide, there would be no problems at all in our educational system.

WE HAD *a fleeting but memorable breakfast at Heathrow as Isobel flew out and Holly flew in. Memorable because we had with us, unopened by order, Holly's GCSE results, 5 As and 5 A*s. Celebrating at Heathrow is not our usual style, but we managed it pretty well!... Holly's summer was one of contrasts. France and Spain with Dickon (Purdue) on a shoestring, in the course of which she acquired and hauled back 5lbs of volvic honey in her rucksack. This was followed by a fortnight languishing on expensive yachts in the Aegean with other beautiful women and apparently rather*

engaging young men. She was impressed by three things: the
earthquake (6.7 on the Richter scale), which she was at the centre
of; the lifestyle, which she found agreeable, and the fact that she
knew more poetry than the Poet Laureate's son, who was one of the
engaging young men.

Many layers of tooth-furring smugness are slotted in there! The letter even includes footnotes, in this case a reminder of the hilarious time that someone in the family brought back fifteen gallons of Greek olive oil – as hand baggage!

Sometimes things do go just a little wrong. Nobody wants horrid things to happen to children, though it can be hard to stifle a smirk:

JACK *is continuing with his bagpipe playing and at the moment*
the house is very quiet, as he is away training and racing in
Italy and Austria. His skiing is coming on well and the highlight
was being chosen for the regional ski team. He skied in the
International Cup in Turkey where he managed to get an individual
bronze medal and was part of the team which won the gold medal
for the first time. He also managed to be in a lift which was
overcrowded and crashed down a number of floors in Istanbul, but
that is another story.

Schools exist primarily to reflect parents' views of their own children.

AMELIA *continues to learn how to play the trumpet, has taken up drama, represents the school in a host of sports, and even copes with cross country running without too many murmurs of disapproval. At a recent parents' evening, it was good to hear how well she is thought of by all her teachers.*

This is from a British family living in the US.

ELEANOR *is a 'straight A' student, excelling in maths and science, but also a truly good all-rounder. She is playing clarinet and was recently accepted by our local youth symphony orchestra. This was an amazing achievement as she is the only twelve-year-old in the orchestra and the youngest by three years... Melanie is also doing incredibly well. She was recently tested and although she's still just eight, was shown to have a reading age of twelve. At a recent parent / teacher meeting I asked the teacher if there were any areas of weakness with Melanie that we should be working on, and her reply was 'no, you've given me a little diamond, and all I have to do is polish it.'*

You might imagine that the return to the UK after time in America might be difficult. Not for our writers' offspring!

LEO *and Cassie had a busy year, which started with sitting exams for UK schools (groan!). They continued to play American Youth soccer (football), both reaching their respective finals. Their karate has improved tremendously, standards in the UK being much more*

exacting than in the US... Leo has continued with guitar lessons
and Cassie is in a local drama programme. They got excellent
reports from their school in Philadelphia, and have made a great
return to school life in the UK. Way to go, Leo and Cassie!

Such wonderful offspring keep at it. They don't let leaving school, their first great arena of achievement, slow them down one bit.

ELIZABETH *is in her final year at Oxford and is president of her*
college law society. She hosted the annual dinner, with Cherie
Booth as guest of honour. Ms Booth was extremely charming, but
gave an earnest and boring half-hour speech. So Elizabeth had an
easy job bringing the evening back to life, and managed to make
the honoured guest squirm, on three occasions. Lizzie also spent the
summer in Vietnam, Cambodia and Thailand.

Of course you know that this account must have come from Elizabeth, the latter-day Cicero, herself. I wonder if Cherie Blair got a thank-you note for her time and trouble.

If nearly all children are perfect, grandchildren can attain almost celestial levels of beauty, grace, skill and adorability. Round robinners love their exclamation marks, or as journalists call them, 'screamers'. Some letters resemble the shower scene in *Psycho*:

PATSY *is now fine, and in all our eyes the cutest, cleverest, and most*
advanced baby in the world!!!!!!!! Just recently she made her first

> *trip to Burnley, flying up with her Mum and Aunty, loving every minute of the long wait in the airport!!*
>
> PATRICK *is nearly as tall as I am (which is not difficult!!) and Pam was overwhelmed with the praise she received about him at parents' night. Is there anything he doesn't do well for his age? The answer is no.*
>
> SHE IS *a complete joy and apart from the first 6 weeks when she hardly seemed to sleep has been an angel-child ever since, full of smiles and giggles, rarely crying, sleeping through the night, eating anything and everything that we offer her. What have we done to be so blessed??!!*

Sold your souls to Beelzebub, most parents would guess. Actually this letter radiates considerable smugness, the writer adding on the next page:

> CAN IT *get any better than this? Living in a lovely house with 'my girls' in a great village community, with a pub which brews and sells award-winning beer...*

With some parents, a brief description of their offsprings' limitless virtues can never be quite enough. This is about a newborn infant ('the most adorable personality we could ever have wished for').

> FOR *those of you who have access to the Internet, Josh has his own website, where you can view the latest pictures and video clips of*

him. Just go to www... and follow the instructions. Email us if
you have any problems.

'Yes, your perfect child keeps appearing on my screen as a pop-up!' possibly.

But all is not without flaw in our letter-writers' Eden. Sometimes children fail to come up to the high standards expected of them. This, however, can rarely be admitted, since, as we have noted, the disappointing children might read the letter. Writers have to skirt around the topic.

> HENRY *delighted us all by getting a first at Wadham. Tibby has*
> *gone the Cambridge route, and has just started to read Economics*
> *at The (!) Queen's College. Susie, well, she is our joy and our*
> *delight, bringing happiness and laughter into our lives.*

Oh dear, learning difficulties there, we suspect. Similar problems seem to have afflicted this family:

> THE CHILDREN *are all thriving. Jack is doing wonderfully well*
> *at prep school, India continues to excel at ballet, and Tara is riding,*
> *both passing exams and winning competitions with flying colours.*
> *Xanthe is eccentric and charming and keeps me smiling.* [uh oh]
> *Kinvara talks incessantly and is a guinea-a-minute!* [another
> euphemism, I fear] *There is never a dull moment, specially since*
> *I dispensed with the nanny in February!*

Or

> EUAN *is doing well at everything he attempts, swimming, football,*
> *martial arts, Beavers, and somehow fitting in schoolwork, to great*
> *effect. All that, and only six. Archie is the light in the darkness.*
> *A more contented, animated, and lovable child we have yet to find.*

Again, you wonder what we are not being told.

Here's another, making it plain which child has performed its duties to the parental satisfaction. Note how the writer has explained precisely how SATs work, so that everyone can appreciate fully the attainments of at least one daughter.

> HARRIET *is sailing through school — works hard and gets brilliant*
> *grades. I saw the entire year's results as they came to the junior*
> *school. She was one of four children, in a year of 250, to get two*
> *level sevens and one eight in her year 9 SATs (that is the highest*
> *possible these days). She was also the only one to get more than one*
> *level eight in her grades for the year, and she got five. For those of*
> *you who are 'out' of education, that is what you are expected to get*
> *when you take GCSEs, which is in two years' time. That is my boast*
> *for this year. She is also lovely, which is far more important*
> *(whoops, that is another boast!). She has written something which*
> *is being used for the Cathedral service I mentioned earlier. Luke is*
> *plodding, still struggling to overcome dyslexia and dyspraxia and*
> *Lauren plays schools when she is not at the real thing! Harriet is*

in the schools' symphony orchestra, and was selected by the county
to try for the national orchestra...

Don't you feel so very sorry for Luke and Lauren?

Often letters hint at something the writers do not wish to relive:

ROSE *thankfully ditched her boyfriend, who was causing us so much trouble last year.*

TAMSIN, *eighteen, is doing so, so well. She is nearly double the weight she was two years ago.*

With so much achievement, so many successes, the orchestras and sports stadia of Britain being filled with the children of our round robinners, it seems awfully unfair that for a minority – admittedly a tiny minority if these letters are anything to go by – things can go wrong.

TOBY'S *life never seems to be straightforward. In addition to his pain – he is waiting for an operation to sever some of his nerves – he has suffered harassment from a previous girlfriend on the course which has, alas, severely affected his relationship with the other students and did not help him in dealing with his pain. He has no shortage of admirers, but is trying to be very choosy after his latest problems. He is looking forward to leaving Loughborough*

University — sadly he has recently had to resign from the special police force there.

This, after lavish praise of several siblings:

PORTIA *is a different matter. She is a hedonist, does not like hard work, and has an inflated idea of her own achievements.*

But at least she sounds nicer than her parents. Sometimes children can let you down in the most unexpected ways.

EARLY *in the summer, Emily's teacher told us that her nose was becoming disruptive and what were we doing about it? The poor child has always been terribly snotty; if you could sell it, we'd be millionaires by now… weeks of nose-drops have achieved nothing. This year's teacher hasn't complained, but I think she's slightly deaf.*

It is rare for these children not to reach the highest levels of attainment. But occasionally it does happen.

MEGAN *is no longer working in the burger van. She now lives with Charlie in Neasden — 'aiming high as usual' said Jenny at the time of the burger van, when she moved in with Charlie to his flat which is in a multi-storey car park (believe it or not!). However, they seem very happy and Megan says the flat is very nice from the front, though we've only seen it from the back, which you get to via the*

rather unpleasant service road, but turn off before the car park
barriers at the entrance.

This last extract is remarkable as the fiercest attack on a writer's child that I have ever found in any of the hundreds of letters which recipients have sent in. But it is also rather magnificent. The last paragraph is, I think, a tribute to the resilience, stamina and sheer bloody optimism of all round robinners:

> THE CONCLUSION *of this year's story is mixed. We may, sadly,*
> *have seen the end of Chloe, having been persuaded to help her with*
> *short-term loans and a deposit to get her new flat. In return she*
> *has broken every promise on the repayments and given us such*
> *unbelievable verbal abuse that we really want nothing more to do*
> *with her. She seems to have little to show for all the money she has*
> *obtained, so we hate to think of what we might have unwittingly*
> *financed. The good news is that we are determined to have a good*
> *finish to the year, so we are off the Dordogne for Christmas, testing*
> *a new caravan! We'll be thinking of you!*

The Stubbed Toe Blackspot

Too much information! That's the cry from so many of the people who shop the senders of circular letters. Take this one from a family in the Midlands. It is more than 6,000 words long, and includes almost an hour-by-hour description of their summer holiday.

> FRIDAY 13TH: *(no bad luck so far!) Pick up euros, haircut, set off 11 a.m., made Dover by 2.20 with no stops, so in time for 2.30 crossing… watched survival and dating shows on French reality channel very similar to programmes at home… leisurely breakfast and back onto the A26 en direction Reims, Metz, Nancy. Stopped at mediocre aire — picnicking was not allowed, so ate sandwiches in the car…*

> SUNDAY 15TH: *woken at 4.30 by birdsong, got up at 8.30, leisurely breakfast. Surprised not to have had a visit from the owners, but I said they would probably come at noon, which they did. We had asked to hire linen as our own wouldn't be the right size, but it was 11 p.m. before we had noticed, too late to bother them… the shopkeeper offered to hold our purchases while I fetched the car, to save Daphne struggling with a heavy box.*

There is disabled parking by the chemist opposite, but we didn't know about it and parked in the all-day pay-and-display for 2 euros.

The holiday proceeded on its uneventful way. 'At 4.30 we hit the village of Vinteilles, and discover – not a lot!' After supper they take out a jigsaw:

UP AT 10.30, *more jigsaw – I did the bit Daphne doesn't like – I go through the whole box and sift all the sky into light, medium and dark, sky with building, sky with foliage, sky with TV aerials; then there are orange flowery bits, orange bricky bits and beigy bits. I could have gone on but it was time to go out... [Friday] we spent nearly all day on the jigsaw: with so many missing pieces and a nightmarish amount of sky we reluctantly decided to give up at 22.30, and broke it up at 22.35.*

But the fun doesn't end there. They go on to Le Touquet where they sit on the beach...

WE CAME *to the (band) aid of a woman who had stubbed her toe, but the next person who stubbed his toe had friends with tissues. It must have been a stubbed toe blackspot.*

The puzzling thing is that if these people came round to your house and described their trip in such detail you might wish to set the dogs on them. But the people who write the letters seem unfazed. Again, no detail of their holiday is too small, including this late breakfast suffered by a Yorkshire family who went to Cornwall:

> THE HOTEL *was largely staffed by surfers, who apparently dictated when they were prepared to work to the hotel owner. Dinner was late one night, possibly because the weather had tempted staff to stay out too long. We needed an early breakfast one morning, because of the need to arrive for the helicopter check-in at Penzance, and it was a very scratch meal, because the dining room did not open until fifteen minutes after the agreed time.*

This concerned an event that had happened fully three months previously. But there frequently seems to be an inverse proportion between the importance of the incident and the way it lodges in the minds of round robinners. This family holidayed in northern France.

> WE HAD *coffee in the old fort, and I bought a stripy jersey, which led to me being taken for a Frenchman at a motorway service station checkout on the way home. While we were in Bronsac we had the excitement of a power cut during lunch. The staff had to add up 'l'addition' by hand!*

But it's not just holidays that come under the microscope. Even the absence of holidays can be described at wearisome length.

THE YEAR *started with snow (and a day without pay!) followed by not a lot until March, when it was visiting time. First, to Bletchley before Johnny and Trish went to Greece, then to Charles and Maggie at Andover. Easter came and went as a long weekend, at home doing gardening etc... for the rest of the summer I stayed local and gave foreign trips a miss this year. Not local was my annual trip to Scunthorpe to see Pru and Pete which coincided and included the Scunthorpe Beer Festival. Most of the beers were new, and made a change from Greene King.*

While some make a virtue of their dreary destinations:

JEREMY *has travelled a number of times this year – but never to very exotic places, mainly Nottingham and Leicester. One trip to Leicester, he managed to stay over rather than travel the 160 miles home... amazingly, we have not gone to Center Parcs this year – somehow think we will have to plan a visit there next year, as we are well and truly CP fans.*

I'll be chewing my fingernails waiting for next year's news! Home décor is also a popular topic:

AT THE END *of May we took the bit between our teeth and started decorating the living room, as we are open plan, this also took us all the way up the stairs and included the upstairs hall. It took us 6 weeks!! Including 3 extra double power points, removing the*

previously filled Rawlplugs, endless rubbing down, lining, painting,
the continuation of the laminate floor downstairs and equivalent
flooring upstairs, yet more skirting and finding and laying carpet
runners…

This work kept the same people away from their other love –
growing vegetables, and of course we need to be apprised of every
shoot and tendril:

DURING *our chaotic life our allotment did suffer this year. As*
usual we have had more than enough soft fruit and vegetables to
keep us going over the next year as well as people avoiding us
during the runner / French bean and courgette / marrow season.
But we only came 39th in the borough's allotment competition,
quite a drop from last year's 5th.

Which leaves the question, why wait until the bean season to avoid
these folk? You can steer clear of them every day of the week! On
the other hand, they are not the only people to imagine that their
plants are of limitless fascination to their acquaintance. Allotments
do tend to dominate people's lives. This is one of only four
paragraphs in a short letter from Wales:

GROWING *your own fruit and veg can be very entertaining. The*
well-established crops, e.g. Jacqui's strawberries, did well, but the
courgette experiment was doomed. The courgette seeds were planted
but only one germinated. This courgette then turned out to be a

cucumber! Next year we will buy courgette plants, rather
than seeds.

Those particular people are exceptional even by the standards of allotment lovers. No detail of their lives is too small to pass on to everyone else:

A GOOD JOURNEY *back to Cumbria was marred by the chronic bottleneck at the junction of the M5 / M6, but it is hard to find an easier alternative. Once back home we collected the cat, who had grown immensely during our holiday. Despite being absent from our house for six weeks, he settled in immediately, with none of the neurotic behaviour of his predecessor. He has grown into a very nice animal, very well-behaved, except in the vicinity of dried flowers.*

Curiously some people seem far more eager to provide you with masses of detail about what went wrong in their lives, and much less information about the good parts. This family in Scotland devote just over two lines to their Caribbean cruise, but nearly four times as much to their problems at the start:

MUST SAY, *the flight to London on BMI was one of the worst we could have been on, and could fill a chapter in a book. Suffice to say the flight was on a rolling half-hour late from 5 p.m., and took off at 7.30 p.m. for an hour flight. On arrival was stuck on the apron for 45 minutes because no parking space... locked in bus for another 45 minutes while driver found construction lorry driver*

who had parked at disembarkation point... not even an apology,
although one steward did liven things up by calling an Italian lady
stupid.

There's a general rule that the people who tell you everything about their holiday will tell you everything about the rest of their lives. Take this family, who flew from Manchester to Majorca. They devote, quite literally, hundreds of words to the cost of parking and the shortcomings of the airport bar, adding on their return:

> THIS WAS FOLLOWED *by the clearing of the bungalow guttering*
> *and the painting of the fascia boards... another time an elderly*
> *friend fell in her flat, and we spent some time in the local casualty*
> *department! We decided to strip down an airing cupboard to the*
> *wood... the washing machine did not qualify for a new door seal,*
> *so had to be replaced... in October we had a bit of a 'do' with the*
> *neighbours... the video of parish footpaths is coming along –*
> *49 out of 62 done so far. The memoirs are up to 1975 – lots of*
> *revelations, and hopefully some red faces if it ever gets into print!*

Heavens, if those revelations are up to the rest of this letter, publishers will be queueing around the block!

Most of us lead rather ordinary lives. What makes the writers of circular letters stand out is their belief that the ordinariness of their lives is fascinating to the rest of us. Take this, from the West Midlands:

LIFE's *not all 'work'. We still go to the theatre regularly — even saw 'Cats' in Birmingham — excellent... We've been to quite a few outdoor shows this year such as the Shrewsbury Flower Show, Southport Flower Show and the Game Fair at Weston Park. I still swim twice a week. This is just a selection of our activities. No wonder I never seem to sit down. I'm exhausted just reading what we've done!!!*

This letter ends, rather sweetly:

I HOPE *I haven't forgotten a vitally important item of news in my rush to get this done. With a bit of luck next year's epistle will report the culmination of the building work and decorating of our house and maybe even the garden. Watch this space!!!*

We will!!!

This next is part of a letter arranged chronologically, sent by a family in west London:

FEBRUARY: *a peaceful month, punctuated by dental check-ups.*

Some use desktop publishing to produce mock newspapers. One from Scotland includes these headlines:

NEW *paintwork in the shower room*
Jemima stars in school nativity play
A summer of disappointing weather
A visit to the Science Museum

That final news story recalls that 'the high spot was the mouse found scurrying among the exhibits'.

Having builders in is exhausting and does tend to dominate people's lives. This is from the West Country:

> WE took the plunge and decided to extend our kitchen, which was something we had wanted to do ever since buying the house ten years ago. It had always been a daunting prospect as we knew that it could ruin the rather pretty back elevation of our house and that two flower beds would have to be destroyed... we decided to have the drive surfaced with tarmac. It was a problem to know what to do without breaking the bank. We hope that it will soon lose its blackness and turn more grey.

This from Lancashire:

> THE gas men finally came on January 11. They were supposed to come at the beginning of December.

Or this, from Hampshire:

> DURING this period and the ensuing months, we converted the cesspit into a septic tank.

Elsewhere there are some exciting plumbing challenges:

THE COMPLICATION *on this occasion was blocked drains to the septic tank which, after hours of rodding, it was decided had to be replaced.*

A QUIET *family style Christmas for 2002? Yes, if you count the delights of installing a new toilet pan and plank-effect floor in our downstairs cloakroom!*

MY FRIEND *Ken came here in the spring and helped put up an attractive wooden roof (marine ply) on the 18ft garden shed – and after waterproofing it looks fine... also, without Ken's assistance, it would have been impossible to extend the landing over the stairs and to fit an extending drop-down ladder for easy access to the loft space. Now, after months fitting a loft floor...*

No, enough! But if you haven't had building work done yourself, you can always fill your readers in on what the offspring are up to:

JASON *and Penny are settled in Norwich and have been making some changes to their house. They now have a conservatory, which catches the sun during the day, and have changed some of their carpeted floors to wooden ones. Jason has insisted that everything that sits on the new floors must have felt feet.*

Occasionally people are so obsessed with building work that they even feel obliged to let the world know when there hasn't been any. This is the first paragraph in a 2002 letter from the south-east:

We nearly *managed the year without working on the house, which was a relief. In October we did have to lay a floor in the utility, as the lino broke up.*

Meanwhile small domestic incidents are often ideal for filling in the otherwise empty pages.

I have *a porch light, which has a sensor, which means that it's on when it's darkness. There is a lot of darkness over the year, which means that they don't last long. Come July 1 I went shopping for another. The first I bought flashed and flickered before it came on. I took it back to B&Q and said it does not work. They seemed surprised, but replaced it with another. That one did not work at all. By this time I was fed up and left it in the hall. For weeks I lived with a dark door, but then I found another at half the price.*

This fascinating tale of domestic life was accompanied by a cartoon drawing of a light bulb, no doubt similar to the ones described in the dramatic narrative.

Here is just one incident from another letter, 3,000 words long:

Our *first catastrophe of the year occurred whilst cleaning the oven; gravity lent a hand and the oven door fell to the floor. I was quite amazed at the distance broken glass can travel, and how it can shatter into such small pieces! ... The second catastrophe occurred when a lighted candle cracked its glass container and*

set fire to the top of the hi-fi/video unit... we now have a scorched
top to the unit, but it could have been much worse.

Then, just as you think that a life so crowded with incident must have some moments of reflective calm:

WE HAD *an unexpected trip to Bristol when Johnny locked himself*
out of the house! His next-door neighbour who has a spare key was
not at home, so not wishing to disturb us, he waited for her to
return. Then realizing his neighbour was away, felt it was too late
to ring us and spent the night in his garage, finally ringing us the
following morning!

Some round robinners' lives are so short of interesting material that they have to predict what they might get up to next year:

A VISIT *to the cinema is in the offing! Any ideas what to see?*

Others make you wonder how tedious a life can be for those who live it to record it and pass it on to others:

JAMIE *stayed and explored Peterborough, which has a Waitrose.*
He can't resist a good Waitrose.

While some are rather lacking in the irony department:

ROGER *has found the website of his old school, and now spends*
hours reading (and writing) about the Penfold Hall Old Boys.
I don't read it unless it's been left on my screen (Roger has his own

computer in the living room) and I fail to see the attraction. They
write trivial rubbish to each other and it is anything but uplifting.
A total waste of time, as Roger never knew 99.9 per cent of the
people who write, but it seems to keep him happy. Give me a good
book any day!

This attack on people who inflict the dreary detail of their lives on others is from a letter of nearly 3,000 words, which begins with a description of the different air fresheners in a B&B they stayed in on the south coast.

But then some people find their own day-to-day lives so fascinating they can't believe we don't want to share it with them. This is part of an 850-word description of the writers' day. It's beautifully printed by computer with sprigs of holly around the edge, bringing a touch of seasonal magic:

Do you have routines? We do. Rise at 07.12 to the sound of
Radio 3, down to the kitchen to make the tea, kettle having boiled
on a time switch. Put in milk until the reflection of the light in the
cups is covered. Take it up to the bedrooms, pour two cups. Turn on
TV and watch Breakfast until the football comes on . . . Janet gets
up, gets dressed and goes down for her breakfast and to make sure
William gets his taxi to school. Used to be free, but now we have to
pay a contribution. Meanwhile I shave with the super Philishave
triple-head shaver Rod bought me for my birthday last year.
Wonderful machine! . . . I weigh out 100 grams of mixed muesli

and Grape Nuts with half a banana and eight grapes, orange juice
and Aloe Vera, read The Times, *starting with page 1 . . . Thursdays*
Janet and I go to Sainsbury's, five miles away. I push the trolley
and pick up things I fancy, choose the wine, while she does the real
work, going down her list and sniffing out bargains. Shopping
done, we have coffee and a bun, or biscuit.

And so on and on until even the writer seems to realize that he
may not be leading the most gripping life:

JANET *read this and said, 'I think we are stuck in a rut!' I replied,*
'well, it's a lovely rut!'

Many fill their letters with photographs, usually reproduced very
badly. Some, incredibly, give technical details: 'Even using ASA
400 film, I needed fill-in flash, as the afternoon had become
cloudy'. Some are the kind of pictures you would throw in the bin
as soon as you got them back from Boots. 'This is us, seen buying
sausages at the butcher's shop.'

Other folk are just anally retentive. Take this couple in
Australia, who use the cheap Virgin Blue airline to fly them around
the continent. They spend almost as long describing the flights as
on what they do when they get to where they're going.

FOR *such air travel we have perfected the art of the in-flight meal.*
Virgin does not offer 'free' food or drink. On the other hand it
allows people to bring their own food. To eat well without littering

> *the cabin, we take: individual portions of a quality brie or*
> *camembert; some cherry tomatoes, a box of Carr's water biscuits*
> *(which are small enough to pop in the mouth — no crumbs), and*
> *for dessert, some fruit. A beer purchased on board helps to*
> *complement the cheese.*

It really does make one yearn to be knocking back champagne and lobster in first class, if only to sneer at their bite-size water biscuits.

Hobbies intrigue the hobbyist, though not necessarily his or her acquaintances:

> THE BEADERS *group met regularly at my house (average, seven of*
> *us) and we explored new techniques, the latest was for Christmas*
> *decorations. Here there was a breakthrough when we found we*
> *could use clear floor polish for stiffening.*

This next extract comes from a closely typed letter of around 9,000 words. It includes the sentence: 'We have accomplished many visits locally, and supported much of the local entertainment our town has to offer.' It also includes this:

> THERE IS *now quite a business in trading railway ephemera —*
> *some steam locomotive plates are fetching five figures. I was pleased*
> *to acquire a working timetable (that is, passengers and freight)*
> *for the now extinct line from Abergavenny to Merthyr and its*
> *branches for October 1912 when it was really busy. Some of the*

> *supplementary information is quite fascinating, such as the*
> *official procedure for cleaning horse boxes.*

Some people feel obliged to record every social event they have attended. This is from the south-east:

> As CHRIS *said, we had a brilliant summer and mine actually started in March / April – the weekly meeting with my Tuffaware supervisor started off with coffee at home, progressed to a beer on our patio, and ended up as two hours in the local pub garden.*

The same writer proves that the spirit of Mr Pooter lives on:

> A FRIEND *of ours has a brother, Les, and sister, Janet, who recently came out as gay. After a few beers (I still don't like wine) at a dinner party, I said, 'I bet you never thought you'd have a brother and sister who were both Leses!' I think I got away with it, we're still speaking.*

Others feel free to record even their most dreadful jokes.

> BERTIE's *middle daughter, Wendy, is married to a Scot of Italian extraction, and they have called their first child Guyano. Bertie asked, in his usual fashion, 'isn't that the posh name for seagull crap?' Fortunately it wasn't in the hearing of the proud Mum and Dad.*

So why tell us now?

Another letter from the Midlands contrived to bore the recipients with news of the Queen, which may take some doing.

I COULDN'T *bear to miss out when the Queen came to our cathedral to present the Maundy money purses to deserving citizens. So dressed 'to the nines' in best multi-coloured blouse & hat & royal blue jacket & skirt I got a ringside place in the Close, chatting to regular 'royal followers' from Liverpool about the cathedral's history while we all waited. I was watching Prince Philip, when suddenly THE QUEEN was right in front of us! 'Good morning, your Majesty,' said my companion. 'You've come a long way,' she said. 'Yes, Ma'am, but this lady lives and works here.' 'Oh?' said the Queen, turning to me. 'Yes, Ma'am,' says I, 'I'm a volunteer chaplain, here to talk to visitors.' 'Very good, well done!' and giving me the most beautiful smile, she moved on. As I said to James afterwards... not much, you might think... but when the Queen of England gives you her undivided attention, even briefly, IT'S A MIND BLOWING EXPERIENCE.*

For the Queen too, I'll wager. I hope she received a copy of the letter.

Jobs can be awfully dull, but that never inhibits our correspondents from telling us all about them. Imagine the tea-time conversation in this home counties household:

JOHN *has consolidated his knowledge of the intricacies of surveying equipment during the year and is still very happy. He succeeded in upgrading the ISO 9001 quality system in March, having beavered away writing three new manuals. The new BSI certificate on the wall makes it all seem worthwhile! Thelma has finally changed her company and she now works for a supplier of tills, or cash registers as you may know them.*

This letter is from East Anglia:

I AM *no longer group marketing manager for Astomia but am Business2Business manager at their light commercial vehicles site on the Diss Road (and in fact my director says he is really pleased about how the site is progressing and in how well we are doing! Now that is a first!) I really loved my job in marketing but felt it was time to move on and all the jobs I wanted to do had a certain element of Sales in them so I thought I would get a bit of sales experience. I also use quite a lot of my marketing techniques at the 4x4 and van centre, and I do enjoy a challenge. Unfortunately the hours of work seem to be longer — the pay is a little better but not as much as I would like. Ah well never mind. So if any of you want a van or a 4x4 I'm your man or woman.*

A surprising element of confusion at the very end there…

Here's another fine example of the curious priorities observed by many round robinners. This letter is nine pages long, but devotes only two lines about the birth of a new granddaughter. However, there is an entire paragraph on the topic of a vacuum cleaner that broke down at an inconvenient moment. It ends like this, on a note that manages to be wonderfully perky and upbeat while simultaneously making the reader want to weep with boredom:

> WHEN *we retired the advice was to keep active, and so we have – just like being back at work! Now we have our Unitary Development Plan – Amendments and the Transport Board's Regional Public Transport Strategy requiring urgent study before meetings later this week. Finally, may we wish you all joy at Christmas and every happiness in the New Year.*

Computers are also a favourite topic. People who love these machines really love them. These folk actually built their own:

> WE WERE *determined that it would be our last and no further upgrades ever!! For you technically minded, 'the beast' is a 350mhz Pentium II with 128 mg ram, 8.4 hard drive with an LS 120 mg floppy drive (5 times faster than the 1.4 floppies), Asus motherboard 100mhz bus, 40-speed CD-ROM, 8mg Matrox graphics card and a Soundblaster Gold AWE sound card...*

Please, haven't you got some news about your plumbing instead? Here's another computer nerd:

I wrote last time of replacing my PC, which was a seven-year-old case with four-year-old works. Those who know my methods will realize the many hours put into developing specifications and checking reviews. The Evesham Axis with AMD 2600 chip won the business... I bought a CRT rather than a flat screen. I am very pleased with it, but for some months it did have problems starting up, until they were diagnosed as a faulty motherboard which Evesham replaced at no cost. After nearly a year I have used 10 gigabytes and have just 65 left!

The preparation of these letters can be a story in itself. One writer records a gripping incident from the previous year:

Last December I was late with this letter... I forgot to take my licking machine to London, so had to lick 80 stamps and envelopes myself, and the glue tasted so awful I had to keep making myself cups of hot Ribena.

Sometimes people in supposedly glamorous jobs also have a dull time of it. Here's a tragic letter from an actor, sent to me by a famous actress, whom I won't name, because she really wishes the chap well:

Having finished playing WisheeWashee in Aladdin at the Pinetree theatre, I had a couple of months to myself [a euphemism for the already euphemistic 'resting'] *before landing two jobs in one week. It started with a Burger King commercial in which I*

played an Easter Bunny and was followed by a corporate video for
DH Evans. Within a few weeks of those, I was asked to take on two
roles in Agatha Christie's Ten Little Indians *at the Grand Theatre*
[in the south-east]. *This was followed by two out of the three*
plays in their summer season, playing PC Nash in The Sound of
Murder *and Clayton in* House Guest. *After that I was cast to*
play in an open-air production of Romeo & Juliet. *This would*
have been a fabulous continuation of the momentum created by the
earlier jobs. Sadly this never came to fruition as the season was
cancelled due to insufficient ticket sales... later I played my fourth
policeman of the year.

It's almost too painful to contemplate. You long for next year's letter to begin: 'Imagine my surprise when, out of the blue, Nick Hytner asked me to play Lear in the National's new production   '

But money can lead to interminable dullness too. One letter starts well, but then descends into rather more than you might care to know about pension schemes:

SEASONS' *greetings! The year began with my father recovering*
from the insertion of a pig's valve into his heart... one pension
scheme (USS) announced that it was consulting its members on
moving from a 1/80th to a 1/60th scheme. I hope they can
implement this retrospective improvement in the next five years...

Meanwhile a farmer feels that Yuletide is the perfect time to update all his friends on CAP support prices:

> SUGAR beet (no acreage subsidy but a quota of 2,400 tonnes at a fixed price of around pounds 30 a ton)...

Cars can also bring out the most tedious in so many people, some because they love them too well, and can talk the torque forever:

> DROPPING the roof on the TVR and driving the cold roads for the hell of it. I am enjoying this. I really like the engine. Nothing clever, an OHV V6, 2.9 litres. It makes a lovely noise and that juicy fat torque makes for swift and easy driving...

But the torque was evidently neither juicy nor fat enough:

> IN MAY I sold the car. It was a great experience. Very much in the big Healey / TR3 mould and now a bit overlooked in the flood of MX5s and MGFs and later, more glam TVRs.

Could one reader in a hundred make anything out of that? Others just like to keep you up to speed on every detail of their motoring lives:

> IN MAY, en route to visit Tom's cousin Rhiannon and her husband in Taunton, the car started making funny noises, and to cut a long story short, we called the AA...

Seven months later, they're filling us in on an engine fault! Why don't people realize that, unless they're talking about a canary yellow 1912 Rolls-Royce, we have very little interest in their vehicles? Few round robinners allow that to slow them down:

JONTY *sold the Rover 214 to Nanette, who is the cook at the village school, with a comprehensive three-month guarantee.*

TOM *now has a VW Polo GT 1991, dark grey in colour, with new alloy wheels and a large bore stainless steel exhaust.*

To HETTY'S *delight, she got a new car in July, a Mazda 323. She polishes it every other weekend.*

MY PERIODS *seem to have stopped, at last. I'm overweight and hope that I don't gain any more. I have been looking for a camper van.*

Others feel a need to speak of their vehicles at even greater length. Here's a family from the East Midlands who travel widely — Cornwall, Wales and even France:

THIS YEAR *we used our new van. This is my opportunity to say a bit more about it. After 30-odd years and two VW campers later, we expanded to a small motorhome (Autosleeper Talisman) which is a 4-berth with toilet / shower, cooker, fridge, heater and all the usual conveniences. This is based on the 2l petrol Talbot Express with a*

GRP one-piece body (no leaks). I used my annual bonus to convert it to LPG (35p/l) and took it to Anglesey for the most competitive quote, and got a weekend in the Welsh mountains thrown in. I have made a list of future tweaks like turbo charger, air suspension, twin choke carb, power steering cruise control but these may have to wait a little longer.

This is from a family who spent Christmas in France:

ON *New Year's Day it snowed and was bitterly cold, I had to go out and move my car, since all Lastide residents must park on the opposite side of the road every fifteen days, but the streets are so narrow that you have to wait until everybody else is ready to move and then do it together.*

To recall a minor parking problem from twelve months previously argues a certain determination. But you might not believe that anyone would go so far as to use a Christmas letter to describe their TV viewing habits. In a way it's quite honest; most people are so busy describing their exhausting charity work, exotic holidays and artistic hobbies that they somehow don't get round to admitting that most of the time they're slumped in front of the box, like the rest of us. Not this London family, however:

I'M SURE *you'll be relieved to learn that we are upholding the good name of the British TV viewing public. Last January we were recruited to BARB who record everything we watch on TV to put*

> *together the national statistics. For the first couple of days we*
> *thought we ought to just watch BBC4 all night long to keep up*
> *the intellectual standard but soon drifted back to watching the*
> *shopping channels… we earn a small remuneration for doing*
> *the service, and have clocked up about £50 so far. We are saving*
> *up for a set of knives.*

They go on to describe what seems to be almost all the programmes they've watched in the course of the year.

> THERE WAS *a feature on 'holding onto the electric fence' and*
> *seeing what happened, which brought back memories to Sally of*
> *walks with her family in the country and holding onto her dad*
> *who was holding onto a live fence…*

Digital viewers should press the red 'destruct' button now.

Politics rarely crops up in circular letters, and when you see what some people write you can understand why. This is from a Labour activist in Yorkshire.

> TASK *Number 1 has been to regroup and get ourselves geared up*
> *to start the climb back. Group agreed a major increase in the self-*
> *imposed levy immediately after the election to continue to fund*
> *regular quarterly newsletters in the key parts of the district. We*
> *are now distributing the third one since the election, which is*
> *better than we did before I became leader, though we still have*
> *some distribution and quality problems. I prepared a detailed*

> *framework strategy for how we should seek to get back in, which has*
> *been agreed by the district party, and we've commenced the branch*
> *by branch initial audit of organization and activity which it*
> *envisaged… I'm trying in effect to get a performance-managed*
> *system in place that focuses effort in key areas…*

This is just a small part of his description of what they get up to in that Labour party. And people wonder why interest in the democratic process is declining! But, as with religion, people tend to proselytize their political views. One man in the Midlands sends a brief note about his year, including just two lines about his son's marriage. This is accompanied by around 2,000 words attacking the new European constitution and a postcard you can send to Buckingham Palace:

> THE QUEEN'S *Chief Secretary, Sir Robin Janvrin, told us in May:*
> *'The Queen has asked to be regularly briefed on the number of*
> *postcards being received.'*

Oh yes, and this year she's taking her summer holiday in Faliraki.

My 'too much information' file is bulging with letters, though some missives stand out as being quite spectacularly overlong. One letter is forty densely typed pages, of which two are devoted to the arrival at his party of a stripogram girl dressed as a policeman. Another comes from a gay telecommunications executive and is arranged in chapters, as if it were work in progress on an autobiography. It consists of thirty-two crammed pages, of which fully four are devoted to his being stranded during a snowstorm – the gridlocked traffic, his good fortune in finding a hotel room, the need to abandon his car ('I moved it to a more prominent position in the car park, so that our security guard could keep an eye on it...') and the train journey back to London. There is also perhaps more than is strictly necessary about his close friendship with a young man he discovers selling the *Big Issue*. But nothing whatever in this man's life is too trivial to escape being mentioned:

> THIS YEAR, *over lunch at the Dew Drop Inn, my Mum was bemoaning the fact that it is no longer possible to phone the local office of the Gas Board. Instead, one ends up speaking to someone in a Call Centre in Glasgow! Mum was saying, 'It was so much better when we could walk into the local gas office in Broadley.' At this point, the gentleman at the next table turned round and asked, 'Excuse me, did you mention Broadley? That is where I live!' In conversation, the gentleman told us he was chairman of the Broadley Historical Society. 'But,' I said, 'I thought Henry Cousins was chairman of the Broadley Historical Society!' The gentleman replied, 'I am Henry Cousins!'*

But the winner has to go to a most astonishing screed, published every year by an academic in Scotland, who sends it to, among others, all his former pupils. He calls this his 'general epistle' and I have been sent what he terms GE5. I estimate that it is 39,000 words – slightly longer than this book. Since it includes a substantial section on every student who has ever passed through his care, no doubt it is of interest to at least some of them. But the letter also includes his musings on cricket, the state of society in general, academic life, a whole page devoted to knotty parking problems, and a lengthy story concerning his landlord and a leaky roof. It is also one of the few letters to include a full page of notes for readers:

> BECAUSE *GE5 has been composed in bits over so long a period, some words of explanation are necessary. Refer to the foot of page 1 and the top of page 2 for the original plan of the structure. Sections 1 and 2 (pages 1 to 36), news of me and the University, were written as they now stand during the period June to August 2002 (though, as indicated in the opening paragraph of page 1, part of it had existed in an earlier version around Easter 2002... as you read these sections bear in mind that allusions in these sections to 'this session' refer to session 2001–02. The ensuing sections, 3a and 3b...*

Aargh! But we may not be alone in our frustration. A German reader, Ulrich Noetzel, wrote to tell me that the situation is desperate in his country too. He received a letter eight pages long, of which he was able to translate only a small part before falling into a deep, catatonic slumber (he doesn't actually write this, but I am sure it must be true).

THIS *circular continues the traditional sequence of the annual chronicle. It begins where the last one ended. Because only the highlights are related, one should remember that usually a year does not consist solely of highlights. Eighty per cent of the time we are at home in München-Gladbach. This circular concentrates on the other times.*

Bring back that jigsaw!

The Pyramids (Overrated)
— and other tales from abroad

NEXT ONLY TO the dazzlingly successful children, the passages in round robins that most infuriate the recipients are those describing holidays. And there are so many. The British middle classes, more prosperous than ever before, with access to the cheapest air fares in Europe, and having seemingly endless free time at their disposal, travel more in a year than their parents probably did in a decade and their grandparents in a lifetime.

And they feel the need to describe these trips, often in the most excruciating detail. In the chapter entitled 'The Stubbed Toe Blackspot' there's a man who gives an account of his holiday virtually on an hour-by-hour basis. If this person were invited round to your house, and commandeered as much of your time to provide the same account orally, you would want to force dry bread down his mouth until he could no longer talk, or even move his jaw. Yet people seem to imagine that this is acceptable social behaviour if it takes the form of a letter.

But at least that person spent a perfectly ordinary holiday, of the kind that two thirds of his readers might be able to enjoy themselves. Others, however, clearly regard the description of their vacations as a form of social climbing, such as this from west London:

> THIS *is going to be a shorter letter than usual; we are preparing to go on a trip to Australia and New Zealand, later today... Travel, travel, travel seems to be the main theme of this year. In September we both went to New York on Concorde; we had flown on it the previous year, for the first time, and we had both fallen in love with it. When we learned it was going to be retired we were determined to fly on Concorde, possibly for the last time. In fact, we flew to New York, and flew back to London on Concorde and absolutely loved it! Since flying on Concorde we have become Concorde junkies... in New York we stayed at the Plaza Hotel, which is very plush. We had a week or so between Concorde flights, so decided to go to Niagara Falls.*

Life must seem pretty empty for them now, reduced to crawling across the sky at a mere 600 mph.

Here's a not untypical letter. You can imagine how a paragraph like this might make the wretched recipient want to track the writers down on holiday and taunt a gorilla into savaging them, or at least puncture their lilos:

> JEREMY *has done so many air miles, he has attained premier status with BA!! It can come in handy, like when he was so held up getting to the airport he still caught the plane, despite arriving*

*at LHR only 10 minutes before departure. We had three extra
special trips. One to Uganda to visit Jen, and sat with mountain
gorillas, AWESOME! One to Washington DC where I got to sit with
John Glenn who was astute, fit, well and still flying his own plane,
great to chat to someone who is a part of exciting history I can
remember happening, and one in Rome where, due to having to
leave early to catch a plane, instead of the group tour of the Vatican
museum, Jeremy and I had a private escorted tour while the museum
was closed to visitors. We do feel very privileged.*

That sounds a lot of travel. But it was not quite enough:

*ON THE holiday front, we skied in January, spent a week on the
Llangollen canal in summer, a long weekend at Center Parcs in
Sherwood Forest (the best bit for me was carriage driving) and
had a long sunny weekend with Pete and Paula in the Algarve.*

It's hard to know which is more tedious – wearisome boasting or
dejection. Here's a sample of each:

*NO sooner back, then off again to France with Tessie and Mungo,
then to Wales with them to visit Tim, who breeds falcons for the Arab
market. Then there was Easter, our own holiday in Tuscany, holiday
in Brittany with Tessie, Jack and Seth, lazy summer days, and
Mungo's baptism party. Off they went, back to UAE. So we had
another holiday in Dorset to console ourselves!*

Alternatively:

> THE YORKSHIRE DALES *were not a huge success, as we didn't*
> *want to walk, and there wasn't a lot else on offer. We did our best,*
> *but we won't be returning.*

Others strain, perhaps a little too hard, to sound sophisticated:

> OH NO, *not another Greek Island! How do we do it? By having a*
> *well-paid wife, that's how! Holidays this year included two weeks*
> *in Turkey on the side of a small bay, voted one of the best views in*
> *the world. Our second holiday took us to the Red Sea Riviera, where*
> *we went to see the Pyramids (overrated).*

Sometimes telling you what has happened is not enough. Some
writers need to describe intricately what they plan to do in the
near future.

> FIRST *we fly to Samoa in the South Pacific before flying to*
> *Thailand via Auckland and Singapore. We plan to stay on Phuket*
> *Island for a few days before moving on to Bangkok. Sri Lanka is*
> *the next stop for 16 days and we hope to see most of the island*
> *during this time. From Colombo we fly home via Dubai for a few*
> *more rounds of golf before reaching Vienna for a short visit, and*
> *then home in time for Christmas. After spending New Year with*
> *family and friends, we plan to fly out to our house in Florida*

until mid-March. Plans for the end of next year will be developing
whilst Winnie is working and we are playing golf.

Can't wait for next year's letter!

The temptation to write too damn much is one that many people cannot resist. Reading some of the letters people send is like being invited round and then forced to look at every single one of their holiday snaps, while listening to a commentary on them all. ('Now this is a bit wobbly, I think I must have been standing on a rocky boulder when I took it, but you can probably see the little statuette of a saint, well they told us there was a fascinating story attached to that…') This next letter, probably fewer than 2,000 words all told, glances over their 'two splendid visits to the States' and a 'Caribbean idyll' before getting down to serious business in Spain and Portugal:

> FIRST *stop was Salamanca, a university town of golden stone with*
> *a delightful plaza mayor. (What better place to have* gambas al
> ajillo *for lunch followed by Ben & Jerry's after dinner, as bands*
> *of students strummed and sang to everyone's delight?)West into*
> *Portugal to Porto, centre of the port wine trade, with lodges lining*
> *the promenade of Villa Nova de Gaia across the Duoro River…*
> *south to Coimbra, old town, twelfth-century granite cathedral,*
> *university courtyard and clock and bell tower… exquisitely*
> *restored* azuelo *tiles depict the stories of La Fontaine's fables*

while the cloisters of the monastery of St Jerome commemorate Vasco
da Gama's exploration... after sightseeing we feasted on frango
no espeto – *roasted chicken, no vegetables...*

Heavens, is it 9.30 already? I really should be getting home to bed.
No, no, I don't need the main course, watching my weight, you
know...

Some people love names, and this is puzzling. Do they imagine
that, even if all their recipients know who these people are, they
have the faintest interest in their cat's cradle of meetings and trips?
This letter, a chronological account of the sender's year, includes
no fewer than twenty-nine different names, many repeated, in just
two paragraphs.

JULY: *Tom and Jean spent a few days down in Frome with Theresa*
and later Tom stayed with Anne, and then went by train to Leicester,
and stayed a week with Carrie. Meanwhile, while Jean gave a talk
about St Francis to a Franciscan Day Centre in Norwich, Theresa
and Jean visited Terry and Anita in their flat in Chippenham, and
later in the month Jean led the Franciscan chapter meeting in
Birmingham in her role as vice-minister for Dottie, who is ill. Pete
has continued to visit Conrad daily. Conrad has moved to a nursing
home. Later in the month we had a birthday picnic for Pete. We
were joined by Carrie and all her family, Theresa and Duncan,
Anne, Justin, and two of his boys, and Terry and Anita... Jacob
stayed on with us, and we took him to the Nene Valley railway on

his way home.

The social whirl continues giddily:

AUGUST: *For our wedding anniversary we got a new carpet for the front room. It is a deep pink colour and looks lovely. We had a very happy day up near Diss with Jean's nephew Tom Parkinson and his wife Jen and their two children Aeldred and Isolde. David and Pat were there and we were joined by Claire and Rob and their two daughters, Daisy and baby Emily, and by Dominic and his Jacqueline. We missed John and Hettie as they had been held up. We got back to the hospital to see Conrad, but he had died earlier that evening. At his funeral we had the joy of seeing Gabriel, who was over from Canada.*

They must all wear name tags. 'Hi, I'm Flossie, and I married Duncan's brother's wife's sister's best friend...'

It is amazing what sticks in people's minds. This letter comes from a gay Anglican vicar, who sends a newspaper including stories about his life:

CROWDS *gasped with shock in April when an Anglican priest fell for a mermaid. However, all was not as it seemed. During a post-Easter break, the Rev. Patrick Brien eagerly made his way to the statue of the Little Mermaid, intending to fulfil a lifelong ambition to see the statue 'in the metal'. He was disappointed to discover that there were yards of plastic barrier tape surrounding the area and*

> *the huge cobblestones on the bankside were being replaced. This did*
> *not seem to have discouraged other tourists, so Mr Brien followed*
> *their example. Unfortunately a quantity of loose builder's sand*
> *proved to be rather a slippery customer, and the good clergyman*
> *found himself having a heavy and impromptu sit-down...*

And so on and so forth, for quite a lot longer.

Other holidays are just baffling:

> RENÉE *and I also had to pull out of the reunion marking the 39th*
> *anniversary of the 1964 student car trip to Petra and Jerusalem,*
> *which took place in Sligo.*

Sligo? Not exactly the rose-red city half as old as time.

And not everyone's holiday is perfect. Disasters come both great and small, though rarely too small to escape being recorded in true Pooter fashion.

> WE VISITED *a small town, the name of which we have forgotten.*
> *Overcast skies changed to glorious sunshine, and I managed to*
> *order a meal at a street café, though I forgot the 'au lait' bit so we*
> *had black tea. They must have seen us coming as I thought 2 euros*
> *a cup a bit steep.*

> BERTIE *was at a Chinese banquet in Beijing, and was seated*
> *between two male Chinese who only spoke Mandarin (and he's not*
> *even fluent in English!) He was using chopsticks very badly. They*

> *sought to be courteous and occasionally put food on his plate from*
> *the rotating glass servery in the centre of the table. He saw sea slugs*
> *on the plate and when they were near him, deciding British cunning*
> *was in order, he would quickly rotate the servery through 10 degrees*
> *so the slugs would pass him by. The courteous Chinese would have*
> *none of this. Sea slugs are a delicacy, and they both served him*
> *some. Of course they had to be eaten. The whole pile of them.*

Some catering establishments have a sign up saying something like: 'If you are dissatisfied, please tell us. If you are satisfied, please tell your friends.' This is not a dictum to which round robinners subscribe, preferring to store their gripes for months before releasing them on hundreds of people who will never be in a position to benefit:

> I DIDN'T *enjoy our summer holiday in Sicily as much as I ought,*
> *because the place we had chosen to stay was supposed to be 4*****
> *and it was not what we expected at all. The room stank of smoke*
> *(I did book a non-smoking room!) and the shower door kept falling*
> *off every time you used it – luckily we had already had our annual*
> *showers! Every time you sat on the toilet seat, you wobbled to one*
> *side and you thought you were going to end up on the floor. The*
> *food was average to poor, and we thought the four-star rating may*
> *have had Mafia connections.*

'I see we had a letter from the Whittles. Any news?' 'Not all good,

I'm afraid. Apparently the Mafia arranged for them to have a wobbly toilet seat on holiday…'

Other people suffer more considerable inconveniences:

WE HAD *a scare after a holiday flight in March when I had a funny feeling in my leg and was sent there as a DVT suspect (false alarm) and then in June Phil decided to have a 'Beckham' injury and broke a meta-tarsal in his left foot. This was incurred not by any athletic pursuit, but by falling down a hidden animal hole while on holiday in France… we had another holiday, in Gran Canaria, where I'd booked an apartment in a small resort via the Internet. The picture on the net turned out to be as accurate as an 'artist's impression' in a brochure, and the apartment was in the middle of a building site.'*

And others suffer even greater disasters. This is from a decidedly grumpy letter:

ARTHUR *had a mild heart attack during a visit we made to gardens just off the M4 to see the spectacular display of red, yellow, mauve, white and chestnut stemmed shrubs. He lay on a bank of snowdrops while a medic administered oxygen before an ambulance took him to hospital in Bristol. He had an interesting week there with Loyd Grossman specified meals. His slow recovery now gives him a good excuse for avoiding social gatherings…*

So we won't be meeting him soon. We can live with that.

With holidays, it seems that all our writers are either glass half-empty or glass half-full people. Some clearly skirt over anything that goes wrong. Others love to dwell on every mishap.

> WE WENT on a cruise to the Canaries while the kitchen got finished, but that was our first poor cruise – the trip to Morocco was cancelled because of terrorism and Madeira because of storms – the QE2 which should also have been there docked beside us in Tenerife instead – the weather was cold and windy all week while England was enjoying a heat wave. The last two days all shops, museums etc. were closed as it was Maundy Thursday and Good Friday. Luckily we had a really good two-week cruise in August – Italy, Greece, Slovenia. Unfortunately at the end, Roderick fell badly on a steep gravelled road in Rhodes and broke his glasses and got a magnificent black eye and lots of bruises and pulled muscles which took weeks to heal.

Going on a cruise is simply to tempt disaster. Take this male traveller. Nothing actually went wrong with the voyage itself, but:

> THE BOAT was chock-a-block, with too many elderly widows on the prowl, lascivious lips all aquiver, slobbering at the jaws, while emitting lecherous snorts and grunts.

That sounds rather like fun. The cruise line should quote him in the brochure.

Or take this, from someone who sounds like a serious grump:

PERHAPS *our most memorable events of the year have been our trips abroad, one of which was disastrous. We decided to spend Christmas and New Year in Italy and set off as soon as term finished. By the time we had reached the halfway point of our journey, it was apparent that I had a serious dose of influenza. We carried on to our destination, a village 50 miles south of Turin, where Amelia's mother now lives. On arrival, I tumbled into bed where I lay with a fever for the next eight days. It was so bad that I even went to see an Italian doctor, who examined me, chastised me for not wearing a vest, and told me I had an enlarged liver. New Year's Eve was spent watching on Italian TV the incredibly duff celebrations taking place at all major cities throughout the country.*

Luckily, on his return to England a real doctor – i.e. not an Italian one – tells him there is nothing wrong with his liver. Phew.

Some people have nothing but bad luck. This family had no fewer than three holidays, all of which went dreadfully wrong:

AFTER *moving mother into her new flat, Maurice and I had a short break in Guernsey at a 4-star hotel overlooking the sea. Our weekend of luxury was something of a disappointment, with two of the three gourmet restaurants being closed or fully-booked, so we had to eat in a makeshift dining room by the swimming pool with the heady aroma of chlorine wafting by. Our romantic breakfasts on the balcony had to be shared with the decorators... our next major event was mother's birthday present, a cruise to Norway and the*

Arctic Circle at the end of June. Off we went to the Land of the
Midnight Sun. Life being what it is, we barely saw the sun at all for
two whole weeks and certainly not at midnight. We experienced fog
and torrential rain... having had one cold, wet holiday and one
where the facilities weren't up to scratch, after Maurice's mother's
funeral we decided we needed a break. Due to shortage of funds we
opted to stay in a friend's caravan in the south of France, and
though we knew the facilities would be 'basic' we thought in
September we'd be guaranteed good weather. How very foolish!

Some people are just never pleased:

IN AUGUST *we went on holiday to Morocco together – to Club*
Med. It was Luke's first encounter with Club Med and he was quite
taken aback that at those high prices he was expected to serve
himself at dinner! He also hated the shrieking microphones. For me
it was a final goodbye to Club Med. The hectic, self-destructive life,
together with the exploitation and the phoniness hit me more
forcefully than it had ever done before.

These people went to Holland to see the bulb fields:

IN AMSTERDAM *we found ourselves billeted in a seedy hotel –*
cigarette burns on dirty sheets and a greasy spoon restaurant –
adjacent to a Sex Museum and lap-dancing bar in front of which
a thong-clad (and not much else!) full-bosomed wench touted for
custom even in broad daylight amongst the junkies and the drug-

peddlers who throng the main street… so on to the bulbfields —
which turned out to be acres of bare earth since they'd lopped off
all the heads of the bulbs the week before our arrival.

This is from a man who had a trip to Northumberland. His 'Most Romantic Moment' came when he played the flute to himself on Hadrian's Wall:

FOLLOWED *promptly by the Least Romantic Moment of 2003.*
I stood up: my trousers didn't. They were caught on the stones, and
the bottom fell out of my world. About a mile back to the car, past
the tourists hooting happily, my neb in the air all the way. No other
trousers in the car. My coffee breaks on the way home were in the
dingiest, most ill-lit places I could find.

To avoid confusion: the *OED* says that 'neb' is northern dialect for a nose.

This next is from a couple who plan to go and live in Greece.

OUR COMMAND *of the Greek language is progressing slowly,*
though our incident with the camper van window tested our
knowledge to the limit. After we'd managed to ease our way into the
van with a lump hammer, we then had to negotiate getting a
replacement window at a local garage. We got there eventually
through a mixture of mime and pidgin Greek. However, we later
learned that the Greek word for 'glass' is exactly the same as the
word for 'mosque' except the accent is in a different place.

For some people you can only feel sorry. These people had planned the photographic holiday of a lifetime in New Zealand:

> I CAME home with 1,200 photos, many of which were ruined, because a piece of mohair off my sweater got caught invisibly behind the camera's mirror. My other camera leaked in light due to the foam seal on the back cover having rotted. Yes, I had checked for faults before I left home.

You can usually find a 3-for-2 offer on Boots' disposables; might be safer next time.

Other people naturally tempt danger:

> JOHN joined an expedition to Cho Oyu, the sixth highest mountain in the world, only 2,000 ft lower than Everest, and no oxygen. It turned out to be a difficult and hazardous trip owing to the atrocious weather. John was one of three chosen for the summit attempt, but did not quite make it owing to severe neck pain. (A blow from a football at base camp had aggravated on old injury.) At advanced base camp, there were two other groups of whom two Germans and the leader of an Australian group died of altitude sickness and two other Australians had to be rescued by helicopter. In John's party one went down lower following a heart attack, one with kidney stones and a Sherpa with altitude sickness. On his return to Kathmandu, John learned that six people had been killed by an avalanche where he had recently been.

One letter is basically an extended account of a yachting trip in which everything goes wrong. Here is a flavour:

> AT THIS POINT *the engine died completely. We were towed into harbour where our passports were confiscated.*

You'd think France would be fairly safe. You would be mistaken.

> FREJUS *was so hot we could hardly move, quite apart from being hemmed in by the forest fires, many of which were started deliberately, that you may recall gutted large parts of France. The campsite down our road was completely burned out on our first night, and at times the fires were too close for comfort. Still, in good British tradition we sat on our patio in summer gear, supping red wine and sampling local cheeses while ash fell from the sky like snow!*

Occasionally those who are lucky enough to live somewhere nice invite their readers along. Not necessarily with great enthusiasm.

> GREG, *Petra, Shelley and James wish you all a very happy festive season, a very happy Christmas and the best of health and luck for the next year, and if you come to Jersey we will get to know about it, so you might as well advise us. Our impression, as a tourist place, it is not great value for money. Great beaches, good scenery, but lacks a focal point, and hotels are poor quality and expensive.*

Others are slightly more welcoming:

> MARGERY'S *legacy allowed us to buy a delightful holiday home*
> *on the Devon coast. Do come and stay!*

But the writer nervously realizes that this might be taken as an invitation to stay for free, and adds: 'very reasonable rates!'

This next must be one of the most disastrous holidays ever recorded in a round robin. The writer lives on the south coast, and he and his wife had used a local paper offer of £5 trips across the Channel.

> SENSIBLE *crossing, no alcohol, arrive in France at noon local time.*
> *To the Market Square for our first couple of drinks, on to a*
> *restaurant for lunch. Visit a couple of bars on our way back to the*
> *boat, and we're in the mood for a few more in the bar on the return*
> *crossing. Now the reason the offer was so cheap was that it was end*
> *of season. Bar stocks run down, so no beer or wine...*

The writer, Dave, buys six tonics from the bar and a bottle of vodka from the duty free.

> YOU KNOW *what it's like when you're pouring your own? You've*
> *got it, not exactly optic measures! After a while, Dave decides he*
> *needs a walk. Next thing, Daph is being called by tannoy to the*
> *information desk, only to be told that Dave has had a serious fall*
> *and cut his head rather badly. We are met at the terminal by an*

ambulance and taken to hospital. While waiting for his head and
face to be stitched, soaked in blood, Dave constantly asks for the
whereabouts of his bag containing passport, camera, phone etc.
Eventually Daph can take no more and decides to go home. In her
wisdom she unfortunately slips, falls and breaks her hip.

She is taken to the same hospital her husband is in, but he, pan-
icked about her disappearance, has discharged himself and has to
be tracked down by the police and returned to hospital.

AFTER *a short while Daph and Dave realize they are in adjacent*
beds. The nursing staff are in stitches (!) Daph is taken to a ward
for an operation, and allowed home one week later with the aid of
a Zimmer frame.

Eventually the bag containing passport etc. is found by a marine
worker who lives 100 yards from the hospital.

WHEN *Mike collected the bag it also contained the vodka. Looking*
at the amount left now we understand what led to our 'downfall'.

Well, that letter has two virtues, unlike most of the others. It isn't
boasting about the writers' wealth, sophistication or resourceful-
ness, and it even tells an interesting story. Here is a holiday that
ended in precisely the opposite fashion, though it too is sad in
its way:

WE ALSO *had a trip to Le Touquet — we must have been the only car returning to the UK with empty bottles clinking in the boot, due to almost missing the ferry and the presence of an over-enthusiastic recycler.*

The Cat That Could Open the Fridge

'THIS HAD us wiping away tears of mirth,' says one reader of a letter included here. It's a long list of accidents and mishaps that occurred to a distant relative living in Australia. They had never met this person, and presumably that is one reason why his endless misfortunes seem so hilarious. People – good, kind people – people who would never dream of laughing if they knew the victim, find themselves rocking and chortling and hugging themselves with delight when it refers to someone they don't know and probably never will.

But it's not merely that we have the capacity to be heartless when we have no connection with the person involved. There is something inherently comical about people who feel the need to describe every misfortune, great or small, that life has sent their way. These people always look on the dark side of life. The effect is cumulative. It's like an old slapstick film. A man falls off the back of a lorry, then is knocked over by a car and drops into a puddle, and the audience – the same people who would rush to help if they saw it happen in real life – laugh their heads off. Take the letter from which this book took its title. The writer lives in Devon. It needs to be quoted at some length to convey the full, rich, tragic effect.

As early *as last November my GP was worried by the high Creatinine level in my blood, indicating kidney problems. Several private consultations were funded by insurance including a kidney biopsy in March which confirmed scarring and damage due to blood pressure that was too high for my body. Pills reduced that, so I was OK for my hip operation.*

Already readers may feel that this is more than they strictly need to know. But the writer is hardly into his stride.

The movement *of my left hip had deteriorated in a year and X-rays in March showed the surfaces of both joints were very rough. The consultant confirmed that there was no sideways rotation of either hip and he agreed to do both together, urgently! In May, before I had the operation, I had to have help with socks and shoelaces but still managed to walk and dance up to the last week, provided I had had some pills. During the op, there was too much bleeding from the first hip so only one was done... in fact my new hip dislocated twice, which meant that I had three general anaesthetics in ten days! The drugs were fine and I had no problems except with Codeine, which caused a bad turn of constipation for a couple of days.*

The writer devotes 930 words of the letter, perhaps two-fifths of the total, to this account of his and his wife's medical problems. It contains many cliffhangers and several false dawns.

By EARLY AUGUST, *I thought I was doing well. However a routine blood test showed the Creatinine was back, and more importantly, I had a very high calcium level. At 10 o'clock the GP said he would fax the consultant and at 2 p.m. I had a call to say there was a hospital bed waiting! I went on a drip straight away, as I was severely dehydrated. Within a few days I was feeling fine and eating everything I could get.*

By now it would be almost disappointing to believe that he was getting any better. Luckily for his muse, he wasn't.

HOWEVER, *the full diagnosis took three weeks of many tests, scans, another kidney biopsy, and a spleen biopsy, which is rather risky but went well... once they decided I have Sarcoid, large doses of steroid were prescribed. Sarcoid is a dysfunction affecting the lymph glands, and can produce a wide variety of symptoms. It seems likely I have had it for several years... I take five different pills a day, with an additional one on Sundays. Aspirin is included, to thin my blood — small knocks make me bleed or bruise. My second hip replacement is due in March.*

Just when you think things can't get any worse, the whirligig of fate turns upon his wife.

SONIA'S *right knee worried me last December as she suffered considerably, then it seemed better in spring, after a fall. During August, she broke a toe by shutting her right foot in the car door.*

In September we both saw consultants and got clearance that I could fly off somewhere. A late booking gave us a nice week on Jersey, until the last evening, when at a Scottish dance, Sonia fell over. She had to drive back to the hotel that evening, and to the airport and home the next day. An X-ray confirmed a broken bone… three days later she had the much-postponed minor operation on her right knee, which confirmed the considerable wear and tear she had. Next she had a nasty spell of sciatica…

That provides just a flavour of their medical problems. The year begins to improve, though bad luck, like an unwanted stray dog, continues to snap at their feet. They ride on the London Eye, but it rains. Next:

GOING to work on one of her few days this year, the car broke down but S managed to drift into a lay-by. The battery has to be an expensive special, as it is under the driver's seat and must not give off fumes. Then one day at the supermarket, the electronic key died, so that was another £90! The runabout I had been driving needed a tarpaulin to keep the damp out of the electrics…

Disasters, great and small, continue.

THIS YEAR Jenny bought a new lounge carpet, but the fitters dropped oil in the doorway… Ben managed to fall off the porch roof in September and is still waiting for a decision on treatment for a broken wrist.

Not quite all is gloom, though. Relatives from Canada arrive. A new computer works well. The children are flourishing, for the most part. But then the letter limps on to its tragic conclusion.

THIS YEAR *Snugs (Mr Snugglekins, our cat) has kept us on our toes.*

(The ones that weren't mangled in the car door, presumably.)

HE *has learned how to open the door of our new large fridge...*

This is the point, on reading the letter, that one is inclined to burst into wholly unfair, entirely inappropriate, and utterly hysterical laughter. On top of all their appalling medical problems, the rain, the malfunctioning car keys, the oil on the new carpet, and every misery and horror that has blighted their lives for twelve whole months, they are faced with every cat- or dog-owner's worst imaginable nightmare -- the pet that can help itself!

One reader has sent in a letter cherished since it arrived in 1990. This too is a seemingly endless list of medical misfortune. To give you just a flavour:

HIP *operation and also the prostate op... very bad flu so I was too ill and too infectious for Tom to visit... back in hospital, in traction, for Christmas and the New Year... I coughed and wheezed with pleurisy and could not get rid of the deep infection in my lung, the doctor had me X-rayed and there was a patch on it!*

> *It took four lots of antibiotics over five months for it to clear up...*
> *after Tom's prostate op they found cancer cells, and the surgeon*
> *recommended another operation... we both felt better by mid-May*
> *but I suddenly developed what turned out to be an acute attack of*
> *diverticulitis (at the time we had no idea what the ghastly pain*
> *could be)... bone scan... arthritis brewing up... rheumatics really*
> *rather ghastly.*

But their cup of woe was not yet full. After this long letter, in which only one paragraph is devoted to non-medical news, the writer adds:

> WE ARE *still reeling over the dreadful way in which Margaret*
> *Thatcher was called on to resign. We think it was ghastly treatment*
> *after all she has done for us...*

But not, perhaps, quite as much as your doctors have done.

After all this it's a relief to find this one paragraph in an otherwise wonderfully chirpy letter from North Yorkshire:

> AFTER *a brief respite last year, Angela's work situation seems to go*
> *from bad to worse. The least said, the better.*

But some people clearly relish the opportunity for a good, long, pipe-clearing, annual whinge. This letter is from a barrister who, in spite of his misfortune, writes from an expensive address in one of south-east England's most expensive towns. The second sentence of his letter begins:

> MY *outstanding fees continue unabated and are still around £200,000. The pressure from my present Chambers was bad in the first part of the year, but eased later on… my new Internet Chambers are doing almost nothing to fetch my greater fees in and the lack of money is becoming a serious problem. My new American Chambers have not made the impact this year that I expected…*

And a Happy New Year to you, too! But this man's life goes on, from dreadful to appalling:

> THE *medical profession have continued their trail of havoc and destruction across every path I tread. They nearly killed the daughter of one of my pupils through a crass and inept misdiagnosis… they nearly killed the wife of one of my colleagues by stuffing her full of painkillers instead of realizing that she was developing septicaemia; luckily the truth came out before they orphaned a six-month-old baby.*

Several similar medical disasters are just averted, or else in some cases end in death. But his life is not all pain. He gives a paper at an important legal conference:

I WAS very pleasantly surprised at how well my paper was received.
It is several years since I have had eminent university professors
queuing up to congratulate me on my academic work!

However, such moments are mere glimmers in the dark forest of
his life. Later in the letter he describes trying to take his mother
to the conference and finding it impossible to get across the road
into the college from a bus stop. This account goes on for approx-
imately five times the length he devotes to his triumph at the
lecture podium and ends, after travails which would have driven
Ulysses to despair:

I KNEW we were in the cheaper accommodation, but I had not
bargained on the communal facilities extending to there being no
wash-basins in our rooms, nor a bar of soap in the entire flatlet and
the fact that the light outside the bathroom needed a new bulb and
nobody had done anything about it...

It takes a certain heroic persistence to recall a missing bar of soap
five months after the event. But our correspondents know all
about persistence. This is the letter from Australia which had the
recipient wiping away the tears of laughter:

TERRY had his two-yearly colonoscopy. They removed two polyps,
but found his diverticular was inflamed, so he had to have
antibiotics for it, he was also going to a physio for a backache when
he fell on the brick pavement in the garden, breaking his right hip

(he had been up the ladder clearing away the guttering, came in
for coffee, then went out to prune shrubs, and fell). We went by
ambulance to the private hospital not far from home, but because
he takes Warfarin they could not operate til the Friday... at the
end of August we were just getting back to some type of normal life
when Terry fell on the tiled floor in the kitchen, did not break
anything, nasty cut on the corner of the eye and huge bruises and
lumps on both knees due to Warfarin... We do not entertain any
more, used to enjoy the odd little dinner parties, we just have tea
or coffee and biscuits. I cannot walk very far because of my back
problem when trying to nurse Mother when she broke her hip, which
she never got over.

What is curious is that amid this medical mayhem, the writer still
finds time to complain that the recycling team no longer comes
round to take away the newspapers. Australia certainly seems to
harbour a lot of poorly people. Occasionally they can blend news
of their ailments in with tidings of the wider world:

DURING the year I have suffered from a prolapsed lumbar disc,
osteoporosis, crumbling vertebrae, bronchitis, colonoscopy, endoscopy
(under anaesthesia), low blood levels, low iron levels... other events
of this year have included the introduction of a 10 per cent goods
and services charge, equivalent to VAT.

From Canada comes a letter bringing yet more medical distress. After a page of gore, including internal bleeding, CAT scans and stomach ulcers:

> I ONLY use my dentures for looks now, because I'm unsure if they will stay put. So I don't go out in public much.

Back in Britain, there are fresh horrors. This man got food poisoning, which set off a chain reaction of blood poisoning, fits, a heart attack, pneumonia and cardiogenic shock.

> THE LATTER is awkward! After being in hospital for another two weeks, Don's recovery is regarded locally as being quite miraculous. Full recovery after such an episode is not possible, and there is some permanent damage. He can recall nothing of the 25 days when he was in intensive care on life-support, nor the week previous to the hospital admission. Shirley, Douglas and Sal remember it very well, of course. During all this they were not encouraged to believe in his survival... Don was soon back at the Citizens' Advice Bureau. He also chairs our Wildlife and Local History Group.

Or take this letter:

> LAST February I had a sudden bout of gastroenteritis and lost two stone in ten days, living on ginger ale and peanut butter sandwiches, when I was able to keep anything down.

Whoa there, too much sharing!

This next writer suffers from depression, which leads him to impulsive acts:

> I DROVE *and drove and drove until I found myself in Lowestoft.*
> *I thought, 'this is stupid. I'd better go home'. So I did.*

Others blend grief and gladness seamlessly:

> MUM *is suffering from psoriasis on her scalp. They celebrated fifty-*
> *seven years of marriage this year.*

So many people seem to take pleasure in their own misfortunes, and pass them round in the way that others share favourite recipes.

> THIS *year has not been a very good one for the family healthwise.*
> *I started the ball rolling by passing out in a chair and being*
> *hospitalized for a week. Justin then had an abscess on his appendix,*
> *closely followed by Julian who had pneumonia... Alice has started*
> *a journalism course and has already had articles published on a*
> *local radio website (she had to give up Equine Studies as she*
> *became allergic to horses).*

This is from quite a short letter, but they certainly manage to pack it full of misery:

> THE YEAR *didn't start at all well. For us the New Year was worse*
> *than usual because we are not devotees of cold, wet, frosty, foggy,*
> *snowy and windy weather... we bought a new car, a Fiat Punto,*

which generally goes well. Instead it didn't go well, and we had to take it back as it was misfiring due to a fuel injection fault. We had just got over this little hiccup when, two days later, the sound of running water was heard and the central heating header tank was found to have a crack in it... we went off to Scotland in the middle of May and experienced a fortnight of rain with only three days of fine weather. We took the car and caravan to the Outer Isles, but £600 is really too expensive, and it does beg the question, all things considered, as to whether Scotland really does want tourists to come and spend money, because we encountered more boorish behaviour than we have ever encountered previously... Derek's blood pressure began to rise to 150/100 and at the end of the year is still high, in spite of beta-blockers... downers have included the new Fiat, which has performed unsatisfactorily, the agents even more so, Scottish weather and some of the natives, a lot of people passing a away within a very short time, and the quite unnecessary public inquiry into the diversion of a well-known and well-used bridleway in the parish.

The letter ends:

ON THIS note, we wish you an equally contented and peaceful 2004.

Which sounds more sarcastic than they probably meant.

Meanwhile some people's children do the suffering on their behalf:

> BEN *saw a string of specialists as by now he was experiencing urological problems and no one could say if the symptoms were related. To date he has seen an orthopaedic specialist, a urologist and a neurologist, has had several scans, physiotherapy, osteopathy and seen a chiropractor, and everyone is stumped. He is very limited in what he can do; heat is the only thing which alleviates the pain… to cap it all his girlfriend decided she couldn't cope with it all, and finished with him in the autumn. This really was the last straw… thankfully Rose ditched her boyfriend who was causing us so much trouble last year… alas, her friend from Grenada has turned out not to be such a good pal, as she is extremely lazy around the house. At the end of the summer Aime went to the doctor complaining of bad headaches, and was diagnosed as extremely anaemic. She is on iron tablets, but as she is a vegetarian, that doesn't help… Jacqui is still working at the Institute, but it failed to get university status after a poor subject review some time ago. All of her department is going to be involved in another move soon to a converted mill, which they are very unsure about as most of the building will be open plan with very little natural light.*

Oh, give us a break, you yearn – quite unfairly – to sigh. Though for some people you really do feel sorry:

This year's main stress has been my neighbours' wind chimes. I can hear them clearly in my bedroom, even with the window closed. It drives me mad. My neighbours do not respond to polite requests, they will not take part in mediation and they are merely indignant at letters from the Council. I am a Quaker and a pacifist, I have training in conflict resolution — well, now I have first-hand knowledge too. I have discovered what hate is, and that I was blessed in not hating anyone for the first 33 years of my life.

And he had a viral infection for four months, including the Christmas period.

It's hard not to sympathize with this chap too:

Rosie had read me some articles in the paper about people who divorce to live with an 'Internet lover'. We were amazed at what seemed to us unbelievable behaviour. Little did we know what lay ahead for us. During October, Rosie found herself chatting on the Internet for hours to a man in the USA. When the relationship came to an end, she was devastated as she had been infatuated with him. We had always felt that our marriage was 'a dream come true' and she swore she would never do it again. She tried hard to stop by removing her software...

Which sounds like some ghastly sexual euphemism...

But she cried and reinstalled the software. On 13 August she left me, and two days later asked for a divorce to go and be with a man

in Toronto. In March this year she went to Canada and married
Arthur! She has not returned to the UK since. The grief experienced
by her mother, my daughters, my parents, not to mention myself, is
unimaginable. The physiotherapy practice had to be sold to meet
the divorce settlement, and the house remortgaged. And I was left
with our two cats.

This is from the US:

DAVID *went to his 20th high school reunion this year and*
returned to tell me that our marriage was over. He and his high
school sweetheart saw each other across the room and their long lost
love was instantly rekindled… that he should find someone else
sexually attractive causes me self-esteem problems that I thought
had been worked out after years in therapy. The pain is almost
physical. He was my third husband and I his second wife, but our
souls were connected. I am trying to be strong, and like the phoenix
rising, I will make my way through this…

This next letter begins with the death of the (female) writer's
mother, and continues in the same vein.

BEFORE *I went up to Mum's we had a visit from my girlfriend*
Emily who lives in the US. She had come over because her elderly
aunt who lived in Warrington was very ill in hospital. Emily
arrived at Heathrow and then travelled up to Warrington. I was
going to Wigan myself to see Mum and Dad and spend some time

with Emily a few days later. (Wigan is only a few miles from Warrington.) We met up a couple of times but saw little of each other because of spending time in different hospitals visiting our relatives. Emily then changed her return flight to the US as her aunt was still very ill, but then there was talk of her aunt being discharged to a nursing home, and Emily rebooked her flight. She boarded the train at Warrington, intending to spend the night at our home in Harrow before catching a flight home the next day. I was, of course, still in Wigan. Sadly, when she got off the train at Watford, she was met by Richard who told her that her aunt had died as she had boarded the train in Warrington. So, as you see, not a good year.

You can say that again. But it was not over yet:

BETTY had a dreadful accident during our visit to South Africa, but I am happy to say she has made a splendid recovery... We went to Majorca for a week, but oh dear, the weather was unbelievable! We were there for just over a day when the storms started. Wind, rain, flash floods, you name it, we got it, and it continued like that for the length of our stay... Tolstoy (our cat) is getting more frail. He never really recovered from his broken leg last year and when he began to lose weight, the vet diagnosed a liver tumour.

The most extraordinary thing about this list of horrors is that it is decorated with little pictures of jolly Santas.

Sometimes people are just too fastidious to describe their disasters in full:

> Two *days prior to Sally's departure on an exciting trip to Latin America, we were visited by two policemen at midnight with the truly awful news that Robert's brother Andrew had strayed from hospital and had been killed outright by a road-sweeper.*

There is no mention of whether the road-sweeper was a person or a vehicle.

This is also slightly baffling:

> So, *apart from Tom's ear, Matthew's kidney, my broken nose, and Fred's castration, it's been a good year. Fred has made an excellent recovery and hasn't actually noticed that anything is missing.*

We assume that Fred is a pet of some kind. But we are not told.

In some cases, you suspect that more is being hidden than revealed:

> We had *an interesting New Year last year with one of my best friends ending up in hospital for a week after a 'domestic' with her boyfriend of the moment. I hope this year's won't be quite as exciting. Jerry spent the early hours of New Year's Day sitting in the kitchen armed with a golf club when the boyfriend went AWOL.*

And what on earth is this about?

JULY *and August were incredibly hot, and on the 21st, right on*
cue, the potato crisp hullabaloo broke out, since when the village
has been at various times in an uproar, pitting brother against
brother, and we still await a decision from the planning authority.

In this otherwise detailed letter, there is absolutely nothing to say what the potato crisp hullabaloo might be.

It is clear that for some people, misery is the only thing that keeps them going. One letter from the Midlands records in detail the anti-tumour drugs the writer, a woman, has been taking. Her cat dies, but there is consolation in the shape of a visit to Coventry. She has to give up working in her neighbour's garden, and can no longer make jam for her favourite charity. Her husband turns out to have Crohn's disease and ulcerative colitis. She ends:

MOST *of my friends are suffering from serious illnesses, or looking*
after others. I hope the New Year brings ease to the suffering.

Here is another letter which is almost, if not quite as terrible as the one from the man whose cat could open the fridge. It begins:

DEAR *Friends, well Christmas is here again, folks, and for us it's*
got to be an improvement on the one we had last year. We had an
awful time with me having been ill since the previous May.
Christmas Day turned out to be no exception, and we were glad
when it was all over.

But there is a chink of hope for these people — only a chink:

FOR *the feline lovers, I am pleased to say that we still have our cat Noodles, but I won't say too much as our previous three cats didn't last long. The first was shot by an air rifle, the second was run over on Christmas Day 1999, and the last one died of leukaemia. The boys were heartbroken.*

The Hairy Archbishop

I DON'T WANT to make fun of anyone's religious beliefs, though it is amazing how many people feel the need to share theirs with everyone they write to. It must be a problem for religious folk. If you truly believe that those who, unlike you, have not been saved are slated for eternal damnation, then the very least you can do is bring them the good news about our Saviour. On the other hand, people who don't share your convictions are liable to ignore the rest of your letter, or even mock your testimony and avowals.

And it is certainly true that God moves in some mysterious ways. Take the woman from near Bristol who recounted this remarkable story to her friends:

> MY *daughter-in-law has been healed of her dreadful eating intolerances. The doctors in the London hospital who have been trying to fathom out the reason for the problem have no answer to what has happened to her. A member of her church told Kimberley that she should visit a church in Bridlington, about eighteen miles from her home. She drove up on her own after a telephoned appointment was made and the vicar and a member of his congregation prayed for her. There was no immediate feeling of*

*any change, but as she drove home again she felt very excited and
very hungry and stopped in a filling station shop. She bought an
Eccles cake, which is something she had not eaten for years, but just
fancied as soon as she saw it. The wheat alone in it should have
been enough to put her in a coma, but she had no reaction at all.
Since then she has eaten everything she desired... her next step is
to try for a baby so we would value your prayers for that to happen.*

Well, if God can manifest His purposes through loaves and fishes,
He should be able to work miracles with a petrol-station Eccles
cake. And the baby should be a doddle. Later in the same letter,
the writer records that her son has been given funding for his
youth work in Yorkshire.

FOR *three years starting last September he had several nail-biting
weeks after not knowing what would happen. His attitude was that
if God wanted him there the funding would become available, and
his faith was rewarded.*

The general idea seems to be that everything good that happens
can be credited to God. But He is in no way to blame for anything
that goes wrong. He is there to see you through the bad times. It
doesn't seem to cross any of our writers' minds that if He can help
you get better, He could presumably prevent you from getting ill
in the first place. Or having that nasty accident.

This is from a British family based in the US:

SHAUN *has continued to be used by God in the places he serves: fire department, church, state government and home... the Lord is using Lucy's gifts through the church, and it is so exciting for me to see. She has also been involved, along with Darren, in door-to-door evangelism this term and she really enjoys that. She has new talents as a puppeteer for the children's ministry at church. Who knew our shy girl could do all these things in public?... So this has been a remarkable year for us. We feel like the Lord has blessed us over and over again. I don't write all this in any way to brag, but only to give the Lord glory for all the ways He's touched our lives through those who have encouraged, taught, befriended and helped us. And to give Him praise for the sights he showed us, the prayers He answered regarding our children and our lives, the strengths He developed in us and the lessons he taught us. We are truly grateful for His grace in our lives! May his blessings surround you!*

The fact that the poor door-to-door evangelist Darren suffered from a severe case of mononucleosis '(glandular fever to you back in England)' is skated over very briefly.

But illness never seems to dent anyone's faith. Quite the opposite:

FOR *some years now Cynthia has been suffering from unpleasant dizzy spells... at the end of 2002 her GP requested various tests because the dizziness was getting worse. She had a brain scan in February, and sadly this revealed that she has a non-malignant*

tumour of the brain. It is in a very difficult place, inside a fold of
the meninges, and the consultant would rather not operate if at all
possible. There is no treatment Cynthia can have because of the site
of the tumour, and so she has to adapt her life to coping with the
side effects. We are so very grateful for our total faith in a loving
and wise God.

Often writers do not see how their assertions of faith must seem
oddly juxtaposed with what happens to them:

DEAR friends, our Christmas wish for you this year is still the
same. Good health, happy days for you and your families, and the
sure knowledge of God's amazing and ever available love and peace
in your lives... Pru finally got her pain and sleepiness diagnosed as
polymyalgia overlying fibromyalgia. The first half of the year was a
sort of blur.

This is from the north of England:

THROUGH all our changes this year, we have known and felt
God's unchanging love and faithfulness, and He has helped us
through the difficult times. The hardest thing to accept has been the
sudden death of Rose's father in July, following a stroke. It was such
a shock, as he had been so active with no sign of ill-health and
Mum and Dad had only been with us a few days before he
collapsed.

Or take this, from the West Country:

> WE *have been in a continuing haze of thanksgiving. Let me*
> *explain. For those who have not heard, Charles had a serious heart*
> *attack during the night last December, and was rushed to hospital.*
> *An angiogram showed a major blockage in an artery so he was*
> *transferred to a specialist unit where he had a tube (stent) insertion*
> *to re-open the valve and repair the damage… our most grateful*
> *thanks to everyone for the loving prayers, phone calls and support.*
> *THEY HELPED US BOTH SO MUCH!*

A Midlands family offer an alphabetical account of what seems to have been rather a mixed year, including:

> *B is for Borthwick Free Church. We continue to be blessed by*
> *increased numbers and faithful ministry.*

> *G is for Grandma. She is as lively and cheerful as ever, in spite of*
> *her pain and disability from the arthritis and the muscle pain she*
> *feels. She can now ride to Tesco's on her Porsche-like scooter.*

> *I is for Ikea* [how did that get in?]

> *L is for Loss. In March we lost an elderly friend of ninety-four*
> *whom Sue had cared for through her involvement with the Tuesday*
> *fellowship. His funeral was a glorious opportunity to share the way*
> *that he had trusted The Lord as his Saviour in his last years.*

M is for the Men's Convention. Stuart and forty others from church joined 4,300+ men at the Royal Albert Hall for a day of Bible teaching and praise to God. As a result, we now have a Men's breakfast once a month at church.

R is for Romania. We visited some friends who were with us for several years at Borthwick Free. Their church is the largest Baptist church in Europe and we once again proved that in a place of material poverty the Lord has chosen to bless in a remarkable way, with true riches.

X is for Xtension! We are delighted with our additional space at church, though it is filling up and we have already had some full houses. Praise the Lord!

Well, we hope you haven't become like zombies as you have trawled through the twenty-six letters above. We want to leave you with our love for a blessed Christmas and our hope that you are trusting in The Alpha and Omega, The Beginning and The End, The Eternal One. He is Emmanuel, God with us! Much love...

Sometimes, though, the Lord's help comes on a more mundane level.

Now, *with my computer resurrected through Jesus's provision of parts, and the help of friends in our Christian Fellowship...*

WE *are waiting for God to tell Trevor what his next job ought to be.*

I wonder what God will say? 'Supply teachers are always in demand, but there's probably more money in plumbing these days.'

But there is no denying that while religion brings peace and happiness to many, to some it brings only chagrin.

> DAD *keeps well and in remarkably good health. The further loss of his sight and the impairment of his short-term memory have aged him — but he is still remarkable for ninety-eight. He enjoys going to the Methodist church every Sunday although he gets very upset that the minister doesn't wear the clerical collar.*

The recipient has scrawled crossly in the margin, 'Blind man upset by "inappropriate" dress code!'

Some people just don't get on with others of the same faith. This is from Lancashire:

> AFTER *an unsettled period of discontent, we finally left our church after more than ten years. We had been unhappy at the change of vicar, and in particular his bullish and arrogant leadership style and lack of emotional intelligence. We gave him one last chance at the annual meeting in April but the whole thing was a charade which failed to see the mass exodus of faithful worshippers as anything other than 'chaff'.*

Another writer does not waste time taking issue with mere vicars:

> I AM *of the firm conviction that Christmas is a festival, which should be enjoyed and celebrated by all mankind, which leads me on to a thought. 'What if Jesus Christ were to reappear in our midst today?' One thing is for sure. He would do a double-take upon our modern day Esau, none other than the new Archbishop of Canterbury, Dr Rowan Williams, who has carefully cultivated an unkempt and dishevelled appearance, which is frightening to behold, and in defiance of the law of Leviticus, wherein it is required that all priests be without physical blemish.*

Like so many modern round robins, this letter includes a footnote, explaining that the reference to Esau is from the bible: 'for my brother Esau is an hairy man...'

Recent events have caused problems especially for Americans, who tend to bombard their British friends with Christian explanations of, say, the attack on the World Trade Center.

> I AM *often asked what God was doing on 9/11. Why was He not protecting and caring for His people? Well, I can tell you what He was doing. He was organising traffic jams near Logan airport, Boston, so that there would be fewer people on the flights that were hijacked. At the same time He was arranging for more heavy traffic in the lower Manhattan area, so that many people would not arrive*

on time for their work in the Twin Towers. In short, He was doing all
he could...

This notion of God as the Fourth Emergency Service seems to be on fairly shaky doctrinal ground. It appears to deny His omnipotence, as well as being rather hurtful for relatives and friends of those who set off early enough to reach the airport or the World Trade Center. Still, no doubt many of those who did lose loved ones will have sent Christmas letters in 2001 explaining how their faith sustained them through the intolerable grief...

A Suffolk reader – a retired vicar himself – writes that he married an American woman in the 1950s and spent many years in the US before retiring home in Britain. 'We therefore receive vast quantities of circular Christmas letters, most of which throw us into quagmires of desperation. Here are a couple of the best from this year's batch':

> THIS *year Moma is spending Christmas with Jesus, looking down on the lights and Christmas trees of Florida, and smiling her lovely smile on all of us.*

> WE *thank the Lord that he has blessed America with the gift of President George Bush, a profoundly God-fearing Christian man of great spiritual depth and high intellectual leadership.* [in the margin] *You folks in merry old England must be so grateful to have Mr Blare* [sic] *as your wonderful prime minister.*

One is reminded of those footballers who pray that God will help their team to win. But then it is startling how many round robinners simply assume that others share their faith:

> I HOPE *that, however hectic your Christmas festivities, you will find room for the Christ Child.*

Another family went on a tour of the Far East and marvelled at:

> THE WAY *God kept us safe both in all our travelling and in our health, and the real sense of His hand was upon us in all our journey.*

This came in the same month as one of those terrible Filipino ferry disasters in which almost a hundred people died. Evidently God was too busy shielding a visiting English couple to pay heed to them.

Oh Dear, What a Plonker!

'I HATE THESE people, hate them, hate them, hate them!' That's a fairly typical reaction to many of the circular letters that wing my way. 'I was appalled by their effusions, as always,' says one recipient, who has, in a fury, gone through the entire letter, which is only one typed sheet of A4 paper, and found no fewer than twenty-seven grammatical and punctuation errors and marked them in a black, angry pen.

It is quite startling how loathed many of the letters are. In some cases it's the smugness, the failure to recognize that other people's lives might be more difficult and more complicated than the bland and prosperous existence enjoyed by the writers. Often it's the blithe assumption that the recipients have both the time and the inclination to plough through thousands of words describing every tiny detail of of someone else's life. When, as is often the case, the recipient hasn't set eyes on the round robinner for many years, the anger mounts to dangerous levels. Some people evidently think that the letters have some evil power that can harm their lives.

I WAS *going to throw this away, but I thought that my waste-paper basket was too good for it. Instead I am sending it to you. You cannot believe the relief I will feel when it is out of my house.*

WE GET *these every year from somebody I was at university with thirty years ago. They are all exactly the same — one and a half pages of excruciating detail about his job and financial situation (including lots of back-biting about ex- or existing colleagues, followed by a cursory paragraph or two about his family).*

Some writers clearly regard the letter as just one of the many ways to inflict their own lives on people who are virtual strangers:

WE SEE *this man only once a year, and we don't know any of his family except his wife. He did, however, entertain us for over an hour at a dinner party with his map and photos, on his laptop, and commentary on their Indian trip. His newsletters generally end up in the bin, unread.*

Often people read letters to the end in spite of themselves.

THE *enclosed is from a friend I knew at university, but whom I have seen only once in the last thirty-seven years. I have never met any of the eleven people he refers to. I confess I felt guilty afterwards about having laughed uproariously about the old lady with one leg 'who we advised to get a ground-floor apartment', and I loved the ending, 'well, you've had your page', presumably reflecting the enormous demand from the Hunters' friends for this offering, which Jim has had to be coerced into satisfying!*

But round robinners are rarely deterred by not knowing their recipients:

THE *extraordinary thing is that we scarcely know the people who have sent it. They lived down the road from us for a couple of years. And we know none of the other people mentioned... but what a bugger those two days of constipation must have been!*

I CAN'T *resist sending this — it's from a cousin who I have seen once in fifty-five years!*

PLEASE *find enclosed a Christmas letter from a friend from the past I haven't seen for at least twenty-two years. The people she mentions I have never heard of, let alone met. Jerry, who she talks about, is her son, whom she left with her husband when he was three years old, and Pat and Di are her present husband's children whom he left when they were children. She writes about them as though either of them had anything to do with their bringing up.*

THIS *woman was a subordinate of mine in a laboratory about twenty years ago. I have seen her probably only once since them. I may not ever have seen her children at all, let alone her friends or dogs... It is an annual saga of a middle-aged Miss Piggy and her accountant husband, their cloned children and their stunningly ordinary existence. Are they blinkered and arrogant, or naïve to the point of gormlessness, or so aspiring upper middle-class as to become ridiculous? I suspect they are completely unaware of other people's sensitivities.*

I USED *to work with this man in Croydon. I expect I never made it plain enough that we didn't want this sort of tosh because it is, in a Pooterish way, often quite hilarious. This year we got two. I believe that qualifies as cruel and unusual punishment.*

I HAVE *never met these people, and my wife's name is not Sue!*

Some senders are clearly oblivious to the rage they inspire in the recipients:

THOSE *who insist on disseminating such gruesome nonsense deserve to be publicly shamed, so I regret your assurance of anonymity. Our only relationship with the perpetrator of this self-important rubbish is that we bought a business from her and the John referred to in the last paragraph (they were then what these days passes for a happily married couple) and they ripped us off something rotten. She seems to think that we ought to retain an everlasting interest in her and her gruesome children. How can anyone produce such drivel and not see that the sole reaction of any sane recipient must be a good, paragraph by paragraph, belly laugh?*

THIS *whole thing is a classic of its kind. The smug, self-satisfied tone and the false modesty are maintained throughout...*

the meeting with 'Sir' Mick Jagger ('we ended up having dinner with him — as you do') and being stupidly busy, constantly disorganized, tumbling on from month to month. Gosh!

THIS man is my oldest and dearest friend, but, oh dear, what a plonker!

THESE people give it to us with both barrels. Roger is boastful, and his wife Caroline is devastatingly crass.

THE amazing thing about this letter is that we have never met the writer. Her partner is no more than an acquaintance, whom we knew about ten years ago when his children went to the same school as ours, while he was in another marriage. Help — I'm starting to produce a circular here myself!

THE enclosed letter was sent to my stepmother. Nobody in the family knows who George and Babs are, and my father, Albert, to whom it is also addressed, died two years ago. We therefore have not the remotest interest in this couple. I'm ashamed to say that our hearts sank when we got to the end and discovered that George and Babs are quite well.

THIS letter actually comes to the family from whom we bought our house, ten years ago. The people who sent it obviously haven't taken the hint of no reply for a decade.

AN *acquaintance of mine, I will call her M, has been sending out self-centred circular letters for some years. They consist solely of a detailed catalogue of her many foreign holidays, about which she manages to tell us everything that is not interesting and to miss out all the many things about the country she is visiting that one might be curious about... I enclose this for your enjoyment, and in the hope that you will dispose of it as safely as possible. I thought you might share my joy at reading that 'the new photos start in volume 4, page 6'. Oh, goody!*

It was certainly hard to get beyond the first paragraph of that particular letter, which picked up from an earlier communication describing M's holiday in Latin America. She leaves her underwear to dry by the hotel pool, and forgets to pick it up when she checks out later in the day:

I GOT *through to the hotel on the phone, but to no avail. When I returned no one would admit to any knowledge of the call, and the owner reminded me that they were not responsible. This then resulted in complicated arrangements to get a replacement bra bought for me in England and posted over to the US. You can't easily buy sized bras in Latin America.*

And did Bruce Chatwin die in vain?

Now and again, for reasons of the purest malice, recipients like to get letters or at least regret missing some. Jude Evans writes from Bridgwater:

> PERHAPS *the most interesting circular letter will be one I never received. A school friend of my daughter failed to get the 3 As at A-level which were predicted. Distraught, she turned to her parents for comfort. The mother's response? She wailed, 'Oh, no! What on earth will we say now in the Christmas family newsletter?' You can imagine what the previous years' letters were like.*

If the writers realized the effect they were having on people they at least think of as friends, or close acquaintances, they would surely never write again.

It is puzzling why people send such infuriating letters. Are they simply lacking in any degree of self-awareness? Is it a socially acceptable form of boasting and status-seeking? After all, nobody would phone someone they had met once in twenty years purely to brag that they were off on a Caribbean cruise, or that their son had got three As. You'd be astonished if you got a postcard in June informing you that the husband of a woman your wife met at a conference in 1987 had just bought himself a new Porsche with fuel injection and twin carbs. Yet circular leters do exactly that.

> WHAT *drives us into a rage is the crassness and sheer idleness of the senders, so obviously using the same word-processor template*

year after year. Same typography, same paragraph structure, the
intro and grinning mugshots, the list of Nigel's latest small-press
non-books, Rachel's dull IT career, their bloody annual Greek
holiday, and the news, with solemn circular vignette, of the latest
relative to 'pass away' (though at least this year we weren't asked
to sign the memorial guestbook on the Internet).

For some people, the letters bring more than just a niggling
annoyance.

THIS *round robin letter from a cousin and her husband (who I*
haven't seen in years, and am unlikely to in the future) does not
just make me sigh with boredom at the banality of its contents, but
lights up a small furnace of irritation and anger that they should
think that I would be in any degree interested in her life, her
family, and of course her numerous grandchildren. My cousin was
constantly held up as the model daughter — so accomplished and
so successful. And, as you can see, she has gone on to produce these
wonderkids, plus a plethora of grandchildren. (I have only one.)
As you can see, this well-meant missile that comes winging its way
can have a devastating effect, reminding one of past failures and
unrealized dreams. It brings up in me lashings of self-pity.

Some writers seem to imagine that the wretched recipients mem-
orize the letters from year to year, regarding each one as the latest
instalment in some gripping serial. Others offer to fill in the gaps.

IMPOSSIBLE *to believe that Christmas is upon us again. For 2003 please re-read the letter for 2002 as we have continued in much the same vein (available on request).*

THOSE *of you who followed our story through to the end of last year will remember…*

One new menace is the Internet. Some writers offer further information on their Internet site, as if the 3,000 words they have already sent is the merest taste of the delights that recipients could enjoy. Others – and this is a growing threat – actually include the appropriate web address for everything they have done, so you don't just have to read about their holiday in Corfu, but can actually flesh out the details with the Corfu tourist board site so you can learn even more about the Brothertons' holiday! To say nothing of their children's schools sites, from which you can download pictures of their offspring as third shepherd, or the writer's employer's site, or even the site for the new car he bought and describes in quite painful detail later in the letter.

So how do the recipients of these ghastly missives cope? In many different ways. Some send them on with enraged comments in the margin: 'Ha, bloody ha!' at some choice misfortune. 'This is the bit that made me fling the whole thing away with a shout of rage and anguish!' One woman tore the whole thing up into tiny pieces, then realized it would be better therapy to send the letter in. She must have spent a long time sellotaping it back together.

One technique popular these days is to send spoof letters to the original perpetrators:

> IN *summer Teddy managed a successful single-handed expedition to the summit of Mount Everest, returning home to find that Darren's new album had just hit number one in the charts. We have had less luck with Debbie, but her probation officer assures us she should be back on the straight and narrow soon!*

'I don't know any of these people, why on earth should I care about their holiday plans?' says one recipient. A writer describes how her new dog is perfect in almost every way, adding: 'His only fault is barking at cars. He is having a healer do something about it.' The reader's comment in the margin is 'I nearly pulled a stomach muscle.' One writer makes the mistake — having described at length his own gorgeous property in Provence — of adding: 'I hope we can visit your own lovely home again some day.' 'Not bloody likely, if this is what we have to put up with!' the aggrieved recipient has scrawled at the bottom.

Another recipient got it off her chest by providing a commentary almost as long as the letter itself. She quotes from it, with her own footnotes, like the concordance to a Shakespeare play:

> 'I WALKED *the Pennine Way with help from my chauffeuse over several days and weekends, and Tim, Tricia and Malcolm who helped out with transport, and D, B&B between the M62 and Ponden*

Reservoir.' Who [the recipient asks] *are T, T, M, D, B&B?' to say nothing of Ponden Reservoir. 'Chauffeuse' is Nick's typical pomposity, and refers to his wife Kate having to do all the donkey work.*

So great is the writer's anger that she hasn't spotted that D, B&B aren't people at all, but stand for dinner, bed and breakfast.

In the same way, others summarise the letters as a means of getting the fury out of their system.

THIS *letter gets longer every year. It's much worse now that some of the children, all brilliant it goes without saying, have grown up and have boyfriends — we are subjected to added news not only about the boyfriends who we have never met, but even about the BOYFRIENDS' PARENTS!!! The formula is:*

1. *Husband is utterly brilliant from every point of view.*
2. *Ditto the wife.*
3. *Both sing brilliantly and we hear an account of all the productions they have sung in.*
4. *Eldest daughter brilliant.*
5. *Ditto next daughter.*
6. *Ditto the son who has moved on from being brilliant with his toys to being a brilliant photographer...*

9. *News of the superb Christmas they are about to have, and*
   news of respective mothers who are, it goes without saying,
   totally wonderful even though frail.

You just know that the poor recipient felt far, far better after she had written all that. One reader points out:

AN INTERESTING *question is WHY don't people have an in-built filter system — as in, 'How does this read? Will it be of any interest to anyone?'*

This reader has spotted the penultimate sentence: 'Our diary is full for the coming festive season, with dinner parties, and concerts, and receptions, etc. etc.' and marked it: 'Pass the sick bucket'.

Sometimes people get their revenge by writing the truth about people's lives in their covering notes.

AN ADDED *irony about this self-praising rubbish is that both him and her are well known for their affairs and casual screwing, so the stories about their happy, settled life are all the more pointless to those receiving them.*

Others, perhaps aware of the distress caused by circular letters, have gone the opposite route. One six-line letter lists various minor vexations in the senders' lives.

As WE *didn't find them all that interesting ourselves, we don't really think you would either. So you wouldn't miss anything by being told all the details. But all the best for the New Year.*

Another says at the top, 'Christmas newsletter, December 2003', and at the bottom, 'All the best, Dave'. The rest of the sheet contains only the words: 'This page intentionally left blank'.

The Whole Darn Human Race

SOME ROUND ROBINNERS think it's a good idea to make their letter stand out from the pack, and they've tried several ways of doing it. Most of these prove to be mistakes. Take the notion of writing up your year in verse. You are not TS Eliot, Andrew Motion, or even Pam Ayres. What you will probably produce is, sadly, not poetry but doggerel. Take this letter from Kent, consisting of forty-four stanzas of a consistent standard, which you can judge:

BEFORE *we move on to the tribe,*
Our holiday we must describe.
We went back to Greece,
Tranquillity and peace
With plenty of wine to imbibe.

For once we were all on our own
The photographs need to be shown
We had a great time
The sea was sublime
With new friends, so never alone.

The last stanza implies what literary critics call a type of ambiguity, in that they were all on their own, and yet never alone. This is either an example of higher metaphysics, or else the writer was short of a rhyme. They go for a speedboat ride:

> THE *driver was grinning with fun*
> *His passengers be spilled, and undone*
> *By shifting his weight*
> *The anchor his fate*
> *Kevin's bulk seemed more than a ton.*

One son has gone into the law, and here the language becomes spare, even elliptical:

> ON FRANCIS *it's now time to focus*
> *But the law seems to be all hocus pocus*
> *Fifty words used,*
> *All are confused*
> *The language was not meant to choke us.*

> *'Tis a conversion course that he's taking*
> *And the second year that he's making*
> *Next year he'll work,*
> *No time to shirk*
> *But the money he soon will be raking.*

This family in the south adopt the same basic form. They have just stopped working:

> So *now John's retired*
> *His hobbies can start.*
> *One day he'll be playing*
> *A saxophone part.*
>
> *He still has his fingers*
> *In several pies;*
> *Sits on two committees*
> *And keeps local ties.*

You sometimes wish correspondents would try to write real poetry; at least you'd feel they'd put some effort into it: 'April was the cruellest month / But Kitty – green fingers! – managed to breed lilacs out of the dead land. She also mixed memory and desire on the Aga and raised £27 for the church steeple fund by selling the result! Well done, her!'

This is from a well-travelled family who manage to encapsulate each trip in a few terse lines:

> *2003 was a very good year*
> *For Withrows and family alike*
> *We travelled again to places like Spain*
> *But not on a motorbike.*

In February our van took us just locally
But England still has its charm
In a Lakeland village we stayed for a while
And rested, safe from harm.

For Sally's big five-oh
We went to a town renowned for art and leisure
We stayed for a while under Florence's spell
And of culture we had a large measure.

Lloyd finally got his reward for hard work
With an MBA degree
Conferred on him at a ceremony
At Southampton University.

This is from America:

THEN, *followed by Chuck Reiss's Volkswagen bus,*
We brought Aunt Ruth back for a visit with us.

Some people seem to feel that poesy is one way they can improve the lot of mankind. This is from a British couple who now live in the US:

BETH *and I went off a-cruisin'*
Lots of eats, a little boozin'
We steamed from California's sunny shore.

Catalonia was delightful,
Mexicanos were politeful.

Soon 'twill be two-ought-ought-two,
There's so much we want to do,
To make the New Year count in every way.
Let us make a better place,
For the whole darn human race.

This next 'poem' is rather unnerving, in that it is devoted entirely to the subject of why the writers are sending it in the first place:

WE have a list of folks we know, all written in a book
And every year when Christmas comes, we go and take a look.
And that is when we realize that these names are a part
Not of the book they're written in, but of our very heart.

For each name stands for someone who has crossed our path some time
And in that meeting they've become the rhythm in each rhyme,
And while it sounds fantastic for us to make this claim
We really feel that we're composed of each remembered name.

And while you may not be aware of any 'special link'
Just meeting you has changed our life a lot more than you think.
For once we've met somebody, the years cannot erase
The memory of a pleasant word or of a friendly face.

For we are but the total of the many folks we've met

And you happen to be one of those we prefer not to forget

And whether we have known you for many years or few

In some way you have had a part in shaping things we do.

You realise, as this unspools for several more verses, that it might be going out to people they met once at a party, or who possibly told them where to find the bus stop. Now they are doomed to receive a missive like this, every year of their lives...

Another well-loved technique among circular-writers is to produce a letter as if written by your pet. This may sound charming, but it creates a problem. Either you keep the whole thing in character, so to speak, concentrating on circumstances and events which a pet might find interesting if it could write, or even think very much, or else you have the pet describe the family's year – in which case it quickly becomes painfully anthropomorphic. This letter swerves giddily between the two. It's from a dog called Micky, who lives with an English family in Spain:

> JIM *looked me in the eye, which usually means bad stuff. 'Why don't you write the Christmas letter, Micky?' OK, I will. First, I want to say something about cats. If you've got a problem with cats, e-mail me. I'll be right over. Second, on the subject of fish-hooks, don't eat them, even if they are wrapped up in sardines!*

So far, in the great tradition of *Animal Farm*, *Watership Down*, *Black Beauty* and so forth. But then we leave doggy topics and move on to a lengthy list of visitors from the UK, local politics, the problems of acquiring residency rights and planning permission — subjects that, frankly, would not greatly concern most dogs. But it ends:

> JIM *says, 'That's enough! Say "Merry Christmas and Happy New Year"'. OK. And remember what I told you, good grub at the skips!*

A family in the north-west have another new wrinkle. Part of their letter is evidently written by their two dogs, as if to another dog in the neighbourhood.

> HI, *Smudger! Can we introduce ourselves? We are the Moorbank House dogs — we live just across the churchyard from you. I'm HIS dog and my name is Arthur   I'm a black Labrador and my assistant dog is HER dog and called Pansy ... of course we're not allowed out of our garden unsupervised so can't visit you in yours — the pond sounds rather fun. However, if one of THEIR visitors leaves a front door open, the temptation for me to go for a walk and visit the Co-op rubbish bags is too great — I'm never popular when I return.*
>
> *Our cats, Sydney (who is the same colour as me and my best friend) and Emily get into trouble over feathered things too. Emily*

thinks she can get round us by putting presents of field mice and voles on our bed, but we don't really like them — too crunchy.

Inevitably the segment is signed with a winsome paw print... Here's a dog that apparently believes in too much sharing as well:

I SAY *it's been a peaceful year, but that's a bit of a lie. I had two dreadful bouts of worms in April and in October. Worms are something I would not wish on my worst enemy — well, perhaps, just on Mugs, that sex-obsessed dog up the road.*

This letter starts in canine style:

HI, *Folks, You may have seen me in that advert where I run around with the Andrex toilet paper, but you didn't know my name — HAMISH... now I have Stripes and the other cats under my control, and I have Derek and June wrapped around my paw! Actually, the only word I can read is 'puppy'. If they try to give me food with that on the label I won't touch it! I'd rather have old dead rabbit, rotting mice or Weetabix — they are really good.*

Delightful though this is, it could get a little wearing. So poor Hamish is soon reduced to bringing us tidings of the household humans.

ON *Friday morning, Tim and Grace were in a car accident and not well enough to travel from Winchester. Alhamdulilah! They are all right but both had whiplash injuries, which take time to go*

away... 19th July was a wonderful day when Neil and Helena
were married. Most of the family were there but not everyone could
make it. D & J enjoyed seeing Neil's godfathers, Jack and Sean,
together again. Neil has left the licensed trade, he says, for more
settled hours...

We seem to have strayed some way from the dog bowl, filled as
it is with rotting mice and Weetabix. But the news must out:

D & J are still playing bridge, golf and tennis. Derek is secretary of
the local show and Grace is chairman of the church restoration
project. They are never bored!

Unlike some of their readers, one fears.

One family from East Anglia, from their letter of distinctly
mystic bent, wrote their annual letter for years as if from their dog
Webster. However, at some point in 2003 this much-loved
animal companion (a Labrador, according to the drawing of him
sporting wings and a halo) passed away. But such a minor devel-
opment would not stop any determined round robinner, and their
latest letter is headlined 'Hello From Heaven'.

IT probably won't come as a huge surprise when I tell you that
these greetings come to you from my new home in the Happy
Hunting Ground. I have to say that I'm immensely relieved to have
moved on at last, and shaken off the shackles of earthly life. As my
old mistress used to say, 'old age is NO FUN', and like her I found

the prospect of discovering Nirvana 'wildly exciting'. And I can
assure you: it is Heavenly! Pastures New are very much to my
liking... now my body lies four foot down, deep in the underworld
in one of my favourite places in the garden, with Michaelmas
daisies and lilies on top and a shark's fin headstone to speed my
night sea-crossing...

Happily, before leaving for 'The Great Awakening', Webster
managed to scratch out some family news.

WELL, *Bridget returned from India as Balambika (having been*
initiated into yogic practices), cleared the sitting room and turned
it into an ashram, only to abandon us all again in search of further
enlightenment, this time in Thailand with her friend James. Her
first e-mails described in detail their bowel movements during an
eight-day fasting cleanse...

It is commonplace for families to give space to every member,
from the oldest to the youngest, to describe their year. This next
letter, however, seems to be unique in being written by a five-
month-old foetus, already named Ben:

WELL, *you haven't met me before. It's a bit dark in here, but nice*
and warm. The only complaint is that I don't have much choice for
the menu, but I'll change all that in a few months' time. I'm
starting to make my presence felt by giving Martha a kick or two.
I'll be leaving my present accommodation around mid-April...

One of the saddest letters comes in the form of a crossword. At first it looks quite jolly, with a smiling snowman and sprigs of holly decorating the top. But it conceals a tragic secret. It was clearly a dreadful year for these people, which you can follow by reading the clues and then the answers:

1. DOWN, *'An insult after years of hard work' (JOB SEEKERS' ALLOWANCE); 2. Down, 'What we often felt' (FED UP); 8. Across, 'Frightening road to freedom' (REDUNDANCY); 16. Across, 'Cheap holiday' (CAMPING); and 9. Across: 'Units consumed increased' (ALCOHOL)*

But of course it ends with 20. Down, 'What we wish you all!' (MERRY CHRISTMAS). For in the world of round robins, being dejected is the ultimate loss of face.

Dining Table for Sale. Any Offers?

IT IS INEVITABLE that the Grim Reaper must visit many round robinners every year. But of course he is rarely ushered in by the front door. Instead he tends to be sent round to the tradesman's entrance, tucked away towards the back of the letter, not permitted to spoil the permanent hectic celebrations in the living room.

> SADLY, *Richard's mother died after a long illness while Richard was in Hong Kong. He could not interrupt the trip, so was unable to attend her funeral. But I feel that the rest of the family gave her a fitting send-off.*

Frankly, you suspect from reading some of the letters, more old people ought to do the decent thing and expire after a reasonable time.

> ROGER's *mother died on the 22nd, though it was really a relief as she had been confined to bed for so long.*

These people want to give a loved one a fitting memorial, and how better than by spending money on themselves?

MOTHER *died just before we were about to go on holiday to the Seychelles. We decided to go ahead anyway, but next year we plan a visit to California in her memory.*

You sometimes wonder how hurt some folk would be if they knew how their shuffling off this mortal coil was shuffled off in turn by their nearest and dearest.

TRAGEDY *struck in August with the unexpected death of Jane's brother Colin. My absence drifting across the Irish Sea in a becalmed race was not helpful. This was exacerbated by a foul return sail from Plymouth with a crew of four, two being seasick and a 20-knot wind on the nose, all the way home. Anyway I had my best ever result, coming 23rd out of fifty-seven in Class 1.*

In spite of this, Colin did not die in vain. He furnished a useful lesson for life:

HE *had sufficient savings to have done many more things than he ever did. So, folks, go out and spend! Your children certainly won't need it, or ever thank you for leaving it to them in your will!*

One letter does at least begin with fourteen lines detailing how the writer's mother died – followed by eleven lines on the passing of their cat. Luckily the family bounces back:

OUR *summer holiday plans were obviously affected by mum's death, but in July we were able to get a last-minute booking for a week in a*

villa in Corfu. The villa was lovely, the weather perfect, and we had
no disasters... this part of the island is very Sunday Times —
apologies to the Guardian, *but the image isn't quite the same!*

It's amazing how a trip can perk people up, even after multiple
bereavements:

> DURING *this period we lost Sandy, our gardener for thirty-six*
> *years (he came with the house) at the age of eighty-three; an ex-*
> *colleague from my firm who died of CJD; and a very longstanding*
> *friend, Tom Rogers, who died from cancer of the pancreas and liver.*
> *By way of compensation we took a day trip to France by Eurotunnel*
> *— very cheap at £9 return.*

Some parents, however, merit only one line:

> IN APRIL *Jim, Jamie's father, died after a short illness — he was*
> *seventy-eight.*

This parent doesn't even appear to have a name:

> JUST *last month, Molly's mother died. Her good humour was not*
> *diminished by the development of Alzheimers. She will be missed*
> *by all.*

This sad single lines come after a lengthy description of an
infestation which damaged the Brussels sprouts in the garden:

> SADLY, *both our new neighbours died within six months of each other.*

Many parents lose any sense of timing when it comes to joining the Choir Invisible:

MONDAY *30th December was scheduled for our New Year family gathering, this time with Shauna and Graham, plus Nicky, Helen, Martin, Trevor and Charles. In the morning the nursing home telephoned to say that Mum had had a fall. Peter went to visit, collecting Shauna en route. Mum seemed comfortable but sleepy, and after a while the pair returned so that Peter could dispense pre-dinner drinks and then carve the largest piece of beef that we had had for years. However, before the carving knife could even be sharpened, the nursing home phoned again to say that Mum had taken a turn for the worse. Peter and Martin rushed there, but too late. She died at 1.20, shortly before they arrived. We became a melancholy gathering, augmented by Pam and Andrew, with no appetite for a house full of food.*

What a waste!

In spite of this, old people can have their uses, if only for recycling all that food:

TIM'S *time is taken up at the moment organizing the bridge club and seeing to the needs of his Mum, who unfortunately seems to have gone downhill fairly rapidly over the last couple of months. However, on Janice's soups, consisting of our leftovers liquidized, she seems to be picking up a little.*

Other mums, however, die in a fine fashion. As you read this you feel the theme music from *Gone with the Wind* should strike up:

> Mom *died a few weeks ago. It was an intensely beautiful time, waiting with her as she died, in her own room in Charleston, in the bed I'd crept into when I felt restless as a child… her breathing was so laboured, struggling to get air through the fluid that filled her body. Her kidneys had shut down. Now the toxins had nowhere to go… Mom hung on as hour after hour passed. I met with the household staff… I told them they could say goodbye. A housekeeper held her hand, brown clasping beige, thanking her for treating her 'with equality'. For her last hour, Mom's bed was piled high with children and grandchildren, singing one Southern Baptist hymn after another and show tunes from* Oklahoma.

Surely they weren't encouraging the old lady to go?

There's a famous story about the Scotsman who puts an ad in the Births, Marriages and Deaths section: 'McTavish dead'. The clerk at the paper explains that he can have five words for the minimum charge, so he changes the ad to: 'McTavish dead. Fiesta for sale.' I was reminded of the gag by this letter:

> After *a long illness, which she bore with little complaint, my Mum died in November. We are now the owners of a fine drop-leaf dining table. Any offers?*

Payment in Canned Goose Liver

THE GREATEST PITFALL of all in circular letters is smugness. It is a trap that only a few writers trouble to avoid. You half expect them to begin: 'Well, it's been another record smug year for the Yarborough family, with smug levels at an all-time high! Everything we have done makes us feel better about ourselves, our achievements and our good fortune, while probably making you feel like an inadequate worm!'

For some reason, Australians can be among the worst offenders:

> EACH time we return from overseas we are reminded just how much we are all very blessed to be living in this paradise called Australia. Long may it continue.

They like to rub it in.

These people were distressed by England's victory over Australia in the rugby world cup final in 2003, though evidently not for long:

> TO the English relos, we thought we had better let you win something. We're happy with the cricket, tennis, soccer, swimming, hockey, rugby league and the weather.

They beat us at hockey too? And we're supposed to care?

This is from a British couple who visited Australia:

> IT's amazing how long it takes to get through customs at Sydney airport when the customs officials ask your wife to remove her jewellery, which is a bit difficult when she's got more jewellery on worth more than the gross domestic product of some small Third World country. And she couldn't get it all off! Eventually one of the feds used one of those metallic scanner things and they let her through — which was a bit of a bugger, because the holiday ended up costing me three times what it would have cost if they'd arrested her.

But complacency can be found everywhere. Here's a woman who uses her failure to ski as the opportunity for a sidelong boast:

> AT the New Year, the four of us went skiing for the first time. I thought that I would probably be okay at skiing, being sort of fit and sort of adventurous. But I found out that I was a skiing wimp, a coward, altogether pressure-on-the-front-footily challenged! However, Natasha and Jack assured me that it was okay, they still loved me. 'You don't have to be good at everything, Mummy!'

Sometimes people's wonderful lives can get just a touch annoying. This family live in rural Yorkshire:

> As we write our annual Christmas letter, it is a glorious sunny, crisp morning as we look out over the fields from an upper room

*and realize we have been at Thornthwaite for five years. We have
been so lucky to have found a place that gives us such joy and the
opportunity for realizing our creative skills, as well as receiving
visitors from far and wide who marvel at the peace and tranquillity
of our home and its surrounding countryside.*

They install an irrigation system from a never-ending spring:

*As the heat of June, July and August bore down on the gardens of
our village, the irrigation system at Thornthwaite paid huge
dividends as the sprinkler systems squirted into action each
evening, both in the flower garden at the back and the kitchen
garden. Much joy and satisfaction was experienced as we gathered
our garden produce throughout the summer and enjoyed the marvel
of flowers planted as seedlings bursting into bloom.*

You find yourself wanting to yell, 'but it's so much simpler to go
to Tesco!'

*TED fulfilled a long-held ambition by going to hear the whole
Ring Cycle in Budapest, with subtitles in Hungarian. His Inuit
book is coming out in Hungarian translation in January, with
royalties paid in canned goose liver.*

Mmm. Make a note to pop round and visit them at dinner time!

But the future of the round-robin letter is clearly on the
Internet. Why bother printing it all up and paying postage when

people can access every detail of your lives by hitting a few keys? A reader sent in a ten-page letter that begins:

> WE'VE been debating the future of our letters. We've had many nice compliments on our epistles, and no one has been rude about them. Now and again Dan receives e-mail out of the blue from strangers who discover the letters <u>on the Web</u> — recently we had fan mail complimenting us on our fifteen-year-old description of germknödel, an amazing Austrian dessert! So, here we go again, with a firm resolve to curb the pen and make this letter shorter. The year, like others, seems to have brought the usual amalgam of family (eventful), music (eclectic), sailing (exciting), travel (exotic), teaching (effective, we hope) and research (erudite) — with some farmyard adventures thrown in. Are we getting in a rut?

Dear me, no. And in case you want to read even more about these people, their letter ends with good news:

> OUR millennium project is to produce a compendium of Christmas letters, dating back to when we started in 1985. We're raiding the family photograph album to get a colour picture for each page. But don't worry: you won't get a copy — there are 150 pages and we can't afford such a large printing. But you will be able to download it from the Net. Watch this space!

Finally, one of the best ways of coping with round robin letters was sent by Alison Davies of Hanworth, Middlesex. As a child she played a game called Winkle's Wedding, in which the narrative was interrupted by gaps in the text. These had to be filled in by the players shouting out random words from a set of cards that had been dealt out to them.

ENTER *the spectre of the Christmas newsletter. One day, while reading yet another missive of fact-laden, self-congratulatory prose, which had fallen smugly from a Christmas card, it suddenly dawned on me that I held in my hand the perfect updated raw material for a reinvigorated version of the game which had thrilled me as a child.*

A few minutes' effort spent writing a list of common, or not so common, nouns on small sheets of paper — a brief glance at this year's shows 'piano-shaped swimming pool', 'truss', 'soggy tissue' — is followed by a businesslike reading out loud of any of these letters, leaving a pause at the right moment. (Try lists of academic achievements, or stories of home improvements.) One of the other players reads out the next word on his or her list. No choice can be allowed; it must be the next noun. In this fashion we have received the news that one correspondent was 'knocked over by an over-friendly CHICKEN McNUGGET', and another's child 'has joined THE THIRD REICH which does excellent work in church and youth clubs'.

Christmas Circulars

This is the season when the myth-makers
play Holy Families – their filtered lives
appropriately merging with the stream
of set Nativities, Madonnas, doves…

'Robert has been promoted yet again!
We're all extremely proud of him, although
it means he has to travel quite a lot.
Sam's football-mad, but passed his Grade 5 oboe.

Jean took an evening class, Renaissance art
– meals in the oven, but we were amazed
at all she knew on our super stay in Rome.
Beth triumphed in GCSE – six As!'

And from the emigrés: 'We came in June…
appalled at how run-down England's become
– no really open space… how did we stand
the weather all those years we lived in Brum?

We have a lovely place near Armidale.
Kate is the tennis champion of her school.
You wouldn't know us, we're so brown – think of us
all celebrating Christmas round the pool!'

They say, between the lines where they regret
there isn't time to write to each of us:
Our life is an accomplishment, a pearl
whose perfect shape and sheen deserve applause.

It's hard, of course. But when we see our lives
reflected here, we're almost led to think
that that's reality. So though poor Jean's
on Prozac for her nerves, and Robert drinks,

and though the children quarrel constantly
and Kate won't eat, and sometimes wets the bed,
and though we often seem to feel the draught
knife through well-fitting doors – it can't be said.

Carole Satyamurti